# The Logic of Love

*Swami Chetanananda*

Other works by the author from Rudra Press:

*Songs from the Center of the Well*

*The Breath of God*

*Dynamic Stillness Part One: The Practice of Trika Yoga*

*Dynamic Stillness Part Two: The Fulfillment of Trika Yoga*

*Meditation: An Invitation to Inner Growth* (audio tape)

# The Logic of Love

## Swami Chetanananda

*Edited by Linda L. Barnes*

Rudra Press
Cambridge, Massachusetts

Rudra Press
P.O. Box 1973
Cambridge, Massachusetts 02238

Cover Design: Milton Glaser
Photograph of Author: Patricia Slote

Manufactured in the United States of America

**Library of Congress Cataloging-in-Publication Data**

Chetanananda, Swami
    The logic of love/Swami Chetanananda; edited by
Linda L. Barnes.
       p.        cm.
  ISBN 0-915801-34-5 : $12.95
    1. Spiritual life. 2. Love – Religious aspects.  I.
Barnes, Linda L.
  BL624.C4525  1992
  294.5'44 – dc20             92-19035
                           CIP

Grateful acknowledgment for the use of the following:

From *The Ruins of the Heart: Selected Lyric Poetry of
Jelaluddin Rumi*, translated by Edmund Helminski.
Copyright © 1981 Threshold Books, RD 4, Box 600,
Putney, VT 05346. Used by permission.

# ACKNOWLEDGMENTS

THIS book is the outcome of many people's labors and gifts. For their work in reading and critiquing its various drafts, and for their feedback on the contents, I thank Kay Andrus, Howard Boster, Arlin Brown, Rachel Brooks, Margaret Bullitt, Sue Farlow, Steven Fenishel, Elizabeth Ferry, Kerry Kaplan, John Kendrick, Helen Leigakos, Melissa Mack, Florence Maddix, Michael Marino, Lorraine Millard, Diana Moller, Steven Ott, Alisa Pascale, Kimberley Patton, Theresa Smith, Duncan Soule, and Sharon Ward.

The creative input of Aurelia Navarro and Nanette Redmond were particularly helpful in the editing process. I would also like to thank Joyce Weston for the interior design, and the graphic production staff at Productivity Press, headed by David Lennon. For their work in marketing, I thank Sarah Fahey and Ellen Hynson. I am also particularly grateful to Milton Glaser for designing the cover.

Most special thanks go to my editor, Linda Barnes, whose care and commitment to this project have made it a fine work.

The work and support of these people have helped to make this book possible, and I would like to express my gratitude to all of them.

# DEDICATION

THIS book is dedicated to my mother and father, whose personal commitment to living a life of love has launched me on my own quest.

Love is reckless; not reason.
Reason seeks a profit.
Love comes on strong, consuming herself, unabashed.

Yet in the midst of suffering
Love proceeds like a millstone,
hard surfaced and straight-forward.

Having died to self-interest,
she risks everything and asks for nothing.
Love gambles away every gift God bestows.

Without cause God gave us Being;
without cause give it back again.
Gambling yourself away is beyond any religion.

Religion seeks grace and favor,
but those who gamble these away are God's favorites,
for they neither put God to the test nor knock at the
door of gain and loss.

— *Jeláluddin Rumi*

# CONTENTS

# EDITOR'S FOREWORD

$T$H E essays in this book are taken from informal discussions, public talks, and seminars given by American meditation master Swami Chetanananda between 1983 and 1991. Some are direct responses to individual questions about specific concerns and situations; others are reflections over time about broader themes and issues. They come out of a dynamic and living tradition of interaction between a spiritual master and his students. These talks also represent a part of the transmission of the teaching which Swami Chetanananda received from his own teacher, Swami Rudrananda, or Rudi.

In one way or another, all the pieces touch on the core issue of this book: What does it mean to live a life of inner mastery and authentic love? Each discussion represents a different way of approaching this issue, whether in the form of opening our hearts, transforming tension, rethinking anger and pain, cultivating nonattachment, or choosing happiness. Each one explores a different approach to understanding what it means to let go — to surrender — and to love.

This book is not a reasoned argument based on a sequence of linear propositions or syllogisms. There *is* no exact progression of steps to take. Instead, it is based on the logic of the heart, a logic which gives us a constellation of themes, all of which are necessary to a deeper understanding of love. Each one grows out of the others; each one helps us see something deeper about the rest. Thus it doesn't matter which piece you begin reading or where you come out, except in this one sense: As Swamiji* has often noted, where you start out is where you end up. So to start with any aspect of love can only take you more deeply into love.

This is a book about the pursuit of love and happiness. It is about coming to know and experience a different understanding of what love is, and of how we can actually live from that state of love. Most importantly, it is about our discovery of the potential for infinite love and unconditional happiness in our own lives.

— *Linda L. Barnes, Editor*

---

* The term "Swami" means "master of oneself." It also refers to his being an initiate of the Saraswati monastic order of India. "Ji" is a term of love and respect.

# The Logic of Love

*Swami Chetanananda*

# Prologue

*The issue is whether we will live with love or not live with love. Our choice is whether to avoid life, or to reach more deeply within ourselves to discover the essential experience of Life Itself.*

# Prologue

SOMEONE recently gave me a book entitled *If Change Is All There Is, Then Choice Is All We've Got*. This led me to think about the basic choice we make in our lives: What kind of people do we want to be, and how do we get there? Who we become depends on the choices we make, and our choices depend on the nature of our awareness. We have to know that the choices we have are real, recognize that certain choices won't take us where we want to go, and have some confidence that our other choices are truly beneficial.

At the most basic level we have two options — two kinds of logic by which we can make our choices and live our lives. One I call the logic of survival; the other, the logic of love. The logic of survival, in all its variations, is expressed in what I call the mantra of ignorance: "What's going to happen to *me*?" This is the voice of the ego. It thinks in terms of "I, me, my" — "*I* want, who's going to do what for *me*, and what about *my* needs?" It is the orientation that says we are in this life to get something out of it. So we can tell that our egos are getting in the picture any time we hear ourselves asking some variation on the question "What's going to happen to *me*?"

This logic of survival takes many forms: desire, ambition, greed, selfishness — even basic self-interest. Whatever we call our particular version, it has the effect of focusing our attention on ourselves in the narrowest sense — which can only take us further into an increasingly narrow way of living our lives. Even the most far-sighted people accelerate their own downfall when they operate according to this logic. Unfortunately this is the logic by which most of the world conducts its affairs.

Acquisitiveness as a way of life doesn't work. The search for love is the search for completion, and we all pursue it. But when we identify love with another person or activity, we are looking for completion *through* somebody or something else. This can only end up falling short, leaving us wondering years later what happened to that love. When we pursue anything outside ourselves in the name of love, we eventually lose any kind of real rapport with ourselves, our lives, and anybody else. The needs we thought would be met by the objects of our pursuit only turn into bigger hungers.

Our egos cannot bring about any change that goes beyond a sense of self-interest. Worse, they function to keep us operating at that level of concern. So whatever variations on the ego's basic question we may ask, each remains only that — a variation on the same fundamental preoccupation with ourselves in the smallest sense.

Furthermore the mantra of ignorance is a question that everyone asks all the time. "What will I get if I do *this*? What will happen if I do *that*?" It comes to us naturally to think in these terms, because almost everything in our lives and our experience conditions us to move in this direction. So any deeper change we want to make in the field of our activity will probably not grow out of the immediate resources of the field itself. *Au contraire.* Any change based on the ego will express itself as some desire to preserve our individual interests. Ultimately, however, it can only end up as one more layer of insult we add to a basic condition of injury.

But is there something beyond our individual existence? If there is, what is its relationship to our individuality and how does it affect our individual lives? To go a step further, what if this "something else" were the *source* of our individual lives — the very essence or energy of Life? I call this essence "Life Itself," and would argue that it is what is most alive about us. It is not merely the source of our individual lives; rather our individual lives are each an expression of this one energy of Life.

There is an internal logic that is intrinsic to the energy of Life Itself — the logic of love. When I talk about "logic" here, I don't mean a science of reasoning or a method of argumentation as is usually understood by the term. Instead I am talking about the limits of rationality, and about a different way of understanding our experience. This is the understanding we discover at work in our hearts. It is what enables us to discern the relationship of individual to individual, and of individual to whole. It is what allows us to make choices based on the awareness of a larger interrelatedness.

We discover the nature of this logic not by pursuing the questions raised by the ego, but by learning to let go of all its issues. In other words, we learn it by finding out what it means to surrender. We learn about the play of this logic when we learn to open our hearts. This is known as finding our center. The stillness we find therein is the source of *real* change.

When we awaken to this potential for real change within us, we can articulate it with great care and discrimination in the field of our individual lives. It doesn't even matter what level of experience we are talking about — physical, mental, and emotional health, well-being in an ultimate sense, wisdom, or liberation. At the deepest level all of these are expressions of the same process of transformation.

The issue is whether we will live with love or not live with love. Our choice is whether to avoid life, or to reach more deeply within ourselves to discover the essential experience of Life Itself. We do this through a practice I call opening our hearts. This is both a technique and an orientation. We learn a technique for opening ourselves to the Life within and around us. As we become more and more oriented toward living our lives from this perspective, gradually we discover that we are not fundamentally different from that same essence of Life.

The logic of survival is the logic of the individual in tension with other individuals. It is based on the very narrowest understanding of the self. In contrast, the logic of love is the logic of the Self in the largest possible sense. It is the logic that takes us beyond all our assumptions about who and what we are — about our individuality, and about how we relate to others.

If we draw upon the logic of survival, we can only live lives of increasing tensions. Then the stresses and strains through which we put ourselves for the sake of accumulation end up undermining our capacity to find any real peace, even on the occasions of our material success. But when we relate in a deep way to that power of Life Itself within us, we come to understand the logic of love, the subject of this book.

When we operate from this logic of love, we find ourselves increasingly able to forego our concern with the issue of "What's going to happen to me?" We develop a broader and broader understanding of what we mean by "self-interest," because we have a bigger and bigger understanding of the Self. We think more deeply about where we come from and where we are going, and realize that what connects these two points is change. Then we have to wonder about the kind of change we want *our* lives to be about.

When the logic of survival informs our choices in life, then our lives become about trying to accumulate people, places, and things. When the logic of love informs our choices, then the process of change we undergo is not about acquiring anything, except maybe the experience and understanding of the deepest part of ourselves.

More than anything else, this second logic leads us into an experience of love that transforms every fear, doubt, and insecurity into creative energy, and our pain and anger into a fullness of life and a sense of total well-being. In real and practical ways, we are able to recognize the highest best interest of all concerned in any situation. We discover that when we live our lives from the logic of love, every change becomes the occasion to discover more about our deepest potential for happiness.

But the bottom line is that *we* choose, and surrender is the key.

# The Logic of Love

*There is a different logic which takes us beyond the confines of our instincts and our preoccupation with self-preservation.*

# A New Starting Place

$M$OST of us go through life conditioned to relate to the world around us on the lowest level available to us: We react to the tension in our environment by getting tense ourselves. For example, when the level of tension in a situation rises, we react by getting angry or more intense. We look for some way to defend our own interests and prove how we are right. Yet however justified we may think we are, these reactions are only ways of becoming closed. Then *we* end up being people who are closed to Life.

Coming to a different understanding of love involves changing this conditioning and learning to respond from a new starting point. In the most general sense this means that, as a situation gets more tense, we learn to respond not with tension of our own, but with openness. We train ourselves to stay deeply open to every situation, no matter how difficult it may be to do so. When we can do this, we find that our own openness has the effect of transforming these situations in ways we never could have imagined.

Staying open is what I call a counter-intuitive response. It means that we learn to go against our initial gut feeling of how we should address a situation — a feeling which usually seems utterly natural and true. So going beyond it is not all that easy, because most of us have learned to rely on these gut feelings, or intuitions.

What we usually think of as intuition, however, is often nothing more than conditioning. It consists of the patterns we have developed as ways of relating to the tensions and pressures to which we have been exposed in our lives. Most of us have learned to trust these feelings. After all, if we can't trust our intuition, then what *can* we trust?

Yet just because these gut feelings seem like something that is intimately our own does not make them particularly conscious or intelligent. The problem with following these feelings is that we stand on our few successes to justify our many less fortunate efforts, skating over all the times that intuition doesn't really pay off.

When we operate according to a counter-intuitive logic, we start out by letting go of our initial impulse. If, for example, our response is to become tense, we first step back. Any tension is really nothing but creative energy that has become contracted. So we look for ways to respond to the situation as a form of creative energy.

A counter-intuitive response, for example, would be to let go, pull back, and start over, looking for a different point from which to proceed. If someone has said something you find unreasonable, you could step back and ask in an open way, "So what do you think would be fair? And why do you think that?" Then you listen, in order to re-establish a real communication and flow between the two of you. In that environment, you have a better chance of conveying what is important to *you* as well.

This is really a matter of taking poison and turning it into love. A real human being takes in every kind of tension — difficulty, frustration, anger, even hatred — transforms it back into creative energy, and returns it as love. This means that when something looks terrible, we don't have to jump down in there with it. We don't have to allow ourselves to be reduced to the lowest possible level within ourselves. Rather we aspire to the highest possibility for all concerned.

Notice, however, that what has to happen first is a stepping back and letting go within ourselves. Counter-intuitive logic comes directly out of letting go — not the other way around. In fact, it is an indication that we *have* let go of some tension within ourselves. This process is not about struggle; it is about learning to become open to Life Itself in all its manifestations and about working to become the best people we can possibly be. This is the spirit of surrender.

# *Giving*

M o s t people's instincts and intuitions run in the direction of self-preservation. This orientation is based on the idea that we are all separate individuals who have to look out for our own interests. This is the logic by which we engage in an endless contest of winning and losing, or what I think of as the game of life. This is the logic of the world, the logic of survival.

The logic of survival grows out of two basic, biological imperatives: the need to eat and the need to reproduce. Rarely do we recognize just how many of our pursuits are one form or another of these two imperatives. We take them so much for granted that it is difficult to imagine not identifying with their demands.

The problem is that this leads us to live essentially unconscious lives based on the shallowest kind of self-interest. Sometimes, even when we think we are doing something different, we are actually camouflaging our own self-interest and just calling it something else. When our instinct for self-preservation dominates us we come up with all kinds of ways to justify serving it. Often we convince ourselves we are giving something to somebody else when, in fact, we are not.

There is, at the same time, a different logic which takes us beyond the confines of our instincts and our preoccupation with self-preservation. It is the logic by which giving and getting cease to be two things and become one instead, and by which our self-interest becomes the interest of the whole — a whole which includes us. This is the logic of love.

When you pursue these matters with some care and depth, what you discover is that the sure-fire way to self-fulfillment is to give your life away — to be selfless. I say this, knowing that it represents a difficult concept. Many of us have a hard time separating it either from old religious training or from years of conditioning in bad relationships. Still it remains one of the most important paradoxes of love.

Let me put it a little differently: If you want something, you have to give it away. That may sound crazy, but it is still exactly how love works. For example, have you ever noticed that when you really want a particular person to like or love you, he or she usually won't? Have you found that when you really need somebody else to love you, you can't find anyone? At the same time, when you don't care about it any more, you've got fifty people standing in line.

There is a good reason for this. It's because two things cannot occupy the same space at the same time.

If you are filled with need, you are not filled with love. So in always giving yourself away, you create an endlessly greater space into which love can come.

An interesting and pragmatic spin on this kind of counter-intuitive logic has been taken by the Japanese, who have taken over whole markets by charging less for certain products. In the short term, they made less money; in the long term, they ended up with much more. So we achieve the recognition of our own highest best interest by learning to go beyond the boundaries of our limited understanding of ourselves and our needs, and by continuously giving all that away.

There is something valuable, rich, and vital in every human being — a spirit that we should respect in others and cultivate in ourselves for the possibility of sharing it for everyone's benefit. Politics won't make the world a better place to live. The military certainly can't make it safer. What *will* make the world a better and safer place to live is when we as human beings attend to that spirit within ourselves which has value, depth, richness, and quality, and find ways to share it, irrespective of what we get back.

When we have that foundation on which to stand within ourselves and when we cease to worry about what we get back, then we are giving because giving in itself is our great treasure. This, of course, is work. It takes real work to direct the energy of our different longings into giving. Sometimes a longing can be so powerful that all we can imagine doing with it is going out to look for something to fill it. Sometimes the longing becomes so complete a reality that we can't imagine there being any other possibility.

Yet if we can be aware of ourselves to the extent that we learn to redirect the longing when we feel it coming, we will develop something incredible within ourselves. Paradoxically it is the only real way to satisfy the longing, because what we are really longing for is to know the deepest part of ourselves. How can anything we pursue outside ourselves possibly satisfy that?

Spiritual practices and philosophies are really only the effects of the enormous effort human beings have made to turn that longing within and to discover the love within themselves. It doesn't matter what vehicle or avenue we choose to sustain us in this endeavor. What really matters is that we *do* it. All the spiritual talk, all the occult jingo, and all the jargon of spiritual groups doesn't amount to anything compared to the simple, conscious capacity to turn that longing within, and find the love within us. *This* is the reality of anything spiritual.

Spirituality is not about talking; it is about doing. In the doing, we find our lives transformed in extraordinary ways. This will not make our lives easier; it *will* in every way make them remarkable.

# A Counter-Intuitive Approach

THE logic of love is a logic of paradox. It tells you to relax when your first instinct is to tighten up. It tells you to let go of boundaries when you most want to defend them. It tells you to stop controlling things, even when you have no idea what will happen if you let go. It tells you to give of yourself completely when you might rather be thinking about how to get something, or how to meet what you think of as your own needs. In other words, it is a logic that is counter-intuitive: It calls you to go counter to all the things your intuitions ordinarily tell you to do.

This means that when you feel like holding on, you probably ought to let go; when you feel like taking something for yourself, you probably ought to be giving. On the other hand, when you have the big urge to give, you ought to think again; when you find yourself chasing after something, you should slow down and wait; and when you find yourself running away from something, you at least ought to turn to meet it.

These are all examples of a counter-intuitive approach. You start by observing your initial, intuitive responses to situations, and then practice turning them around. It is not that you have to make a whole-hearted commitment in every case to do what runs counter to your intuition, but you do have to be aware of how you are responding to a situation, and check whether your response and reactions are really promoting the benefit of the whole.

From the point of view of the logic of love, our initial responses often actually undermine our capacity to be loving people and to extend our awareness of love into our lives. It is amazing how much we unconsciously allow our individual issues to override any awareness we might have of being open and loving in a larger sense — and we do so all in the name of love.

Therefore a real part of your inner work involves observing your own behavior. It involves looking at what you do to promote a flow of creative energy in a situation, and what you do to obstruct it. When I refer to this flow of energy and how it operates, I am really talking first about how you free a sense of flow within yourself and then about how you extend it throughout the whole field of your life. If you are to become aware of the wholeness of Life Itself and its vitality — an awareness, in other words, of love — then an integration of your inner and outer experience has to take place.

It is an important part of your inner work to learn to connect to your own center and to the flow of your creative energy not just in certain intense areas of your life, but in every area. This is the challenge for all of us, and I will talk more about how to do it in the next part of the book.

There is no thinking or reasoning our way through the challenges in our lives, either. This is because of the nature of the mind, whose favorite question is some variation on the all-time favorite human theme-song, "What's Going to Happen to Me?" So once we find ourselves trying to *think* these things through, we tend to get lost in that question. Any answer we come up with is going to have little to do with real love, and more to do with some form of self-interest.

I said that the logic of love is a logic of paradox. The only way to the other side of a paradox has nothing to do with any of the means we ordinarily use in problem-solving. For example, it has nothing to do with resisting the problem or with reasoning our way through it. The only way to resolve a paradox is by learning to open our hearts and let go — to surrender.

All paradox is resolved in surrender. When we learn to open our hearts to a situation and let go of what we think we need or want to have happen, then we are no longer overcome by our experience of tension, uncertainty, or isolation. Our deepest creative resource comes into play, releasing the capacity for creative energy, freedom, and unconditional happiness inherent in each of us. These not only take us to love; they *are* the qualities of love.

In an atmosphere free of desire, free of motive, and free of purpose, we are established in love. Established in that experience of love, the most difficult giving we ever have to do turns into an incredible joy and a great expansion. We find that the hardest things we ever have to give up become things which only increase us. This is the logic of paradox and the nature of love. It is what happens when we learn to open our hearts.

# Opening Our Hearts

Learning to open your heart is like learning to play an instrument. You start out with a basic exercise, and practice that over and over again until you have mastered it. Gradually you find that your whole experience of the music you play has changed.

# Surrender

*T*HE challenge we all face in our lives is to open our hearts first to ourselves, and then to the people with whom we share our lives every single day. We cultivate the strength, the refinement and, most importantly, the wisdom that comes from knowing our own hearts deeply. This is the same thing as knowing what it is to love. As we learn what it is to be full of love, and as the joy of that fullness overflows in us, we can share it with whoever wants it. In fact, that sharing will simply happen of its own accord.

In learning to open our hearts to Life, we learn to let go of the many ways we are conditioned to respond and react to the people and events around us. Learning to respond differently takes a lot of inner work, so letting go of our conditioning is where the issue of surrender comes into the picture. We undertake this inner work because of what *we* become as a result: people established in love, for whom even the tensions and difficulties of life are the occasion to learn more and more about love.

Often when we hear the word "surrender" we think that it means losing something in a conflict, or having to give up something under pressure. We think about it as some kind of defeat, submission, or the loss of something important. We worry about what it's going to mean in our own lives, and about what *we* are going to have to give up. In general, it becomes a term we associate with our loss and someone else's gain. So it can be a difficult concept for many of us to accept.

In relation to inner mastery, however, surrender means something very different. In this regard, it has nothing to do with losing anything except what we can well afford to give up in the first place. There is no defeat, no submission, no real loss. It is my experience that in inner work the only things we have to surrender are what we perceive to be our limitations. For example, my teacher Rudi used to say, "The only thing you have to give up is your guilt." That's not so hard to live with.

Surrender is what happens every time we open our hearts and practice living in that spirit of openness. When I say "opening our hearts," I am talking both about a general principle and a simple practice we can learn to do. Opening our hearts starts out as a technique that we can do every day, under any and all circumstances. With practice, it develops into an awareness that informs how we see all of life.

Eventually, we become able to move through our everyday lives and face the challenges we must, even as we sustain that awareness. The process of learning how to do this is what begins to open up our understanding of who and what we are in relation to Life Itself.

# Tension and Creative Energy

We all start out with fundamentally open hearts. We are, by nature, open. Yet as we interact with the world and experience various disappointments, slowly a compression and crusting over sets in and we close up. When we practice consciously opening our hearts again, this crystallization begins to break down into its original element, which is creative energy.

As we recover this creative energy, we begin to see that *it* is what we really are. Initially we will experience this process as a kind of agitation. What it really is, however, is an intensification of our energy. We are getting back energy that has been tied up in tension.

I am using the word "tension" as a generic term that includes any sense of inner contraction. In this context, anger is tension, as are fear, doubt, and insecurity. Many of us are more aware of these as individual kinds of tension, but what I am talking about is a more comprehensive way of thinking about them. I am suggesting what it is they all have in common. In a fundamental sense, each of these different feelings represents a contraction of our creative energy.

Closing our hearts brings about what I call "crystallization." Crystallization refers to the hardness, the crust — the tension — that sets up in our hearts as we go through our lives. We may experience it as some form of fear, doubt, or anxiety. The really frightening thing, however, is that as we go through our lives this crystallization happens so slowly that we often don't even notice it. We assume that it constitutes part of our basic condition.

Usually we want to explain each feeling that we have. We want to identify our tension as one thing or another — as fear or anger or some other strong emotion. We lose sight of the fact that growth and change cannot happen without a certain amount of internal reorganization or agitation. But if we put a name on this process of reorganization, we limit it. Then, instead of simply sitting through it, we have to react to it and *do* something about it.

Once we think that our tension is fear or anger, for example, we make the fear or anger the reality when neither of them has to be. The truth is that tension is not really fear or anger or anything else; it is just an opportunity to override the impulse to close our hearts, and to allow our energy to reorganize itself in a process of real inner change and growth.

The minute we feel some kind of life waking up in us, we often want to step on it right away. That's what all our reactions are. Yet instead of crushing the change that is trying to happen, the real point is just to sit with it. We do this by keeping still, becoming centered, and staying open through all the change. Refusing to react to Life or close ourselves off to it, instead we just let it unfold.

# The Basic Exercise

*L*EARNING to open your heart starts out as a simple technique, the deeper meaning of which evolves with practice over time. It is like learning to play an instrument. You start out with a basic exercise, and practice that over and over again until you have mastered it. Gradually you find that your whole experience of the music you play changes.

When I talk about opening your heart, I am not talking about the muscle in your chest. Rather I mean a profound energy center from and through which your inner spirit functions. We have all experienced that center. Think, for example, of the times you felt your heart was broken. That experience had nothing to do with your physical heart, and yet you may have felt a very real pain in your chest. What was contracting was this center of energy.

It is possible, through practice, to become familiar with this center in this way: Start by sitting down in a quiet place and becoming quiet. Breathing naturally, take a deep breath into your upper chest, filling the whole cavity with air. When your upper chest is filled, your breath will naturally pause and hold. At that point, take your attention inside, directing it into the center of your chest in the area of your heart. Then wait a moment. As you do so, deeply ask to grow. Repeat this process as you continue breathing deeply and quietly.

At first you will probably feel that area get a little bit tight. It may even feel as though it's starting to crack. If you stay with it, though, and keep asking to grow, it will first start to relax and expand, and then it will open. (If you can't feel this right away, don't worry about it. Simply continue to practice regularly.) As you experience this sense of expansion, notice two things: a subtle spinning or vibrating, and a feeling of quiet sweetness that begins to unfold.

This is the basic meditation exercise for opening your heart. You can do this alone, or sitting in the company of others. Eventually, you will become skilled at doing it in the midst of your interactions with the world around you.

This exercise may sound simple, but if you practice doing it on a regular basis, you will experience something deeper start to happen. For one thing, your body will become less a feature of your awareness as your attention moves to something deeper. For another, your mind and its activity will become a less prominent part of your awareness and you won't notice your thoughts in the same way.

Notice, too, how your experience of your physical boundaries changes, becoming bigger and more open. Until we begin to learn new ways to experience ourselves, we usually have no alternative frame of reference from which to see that what we take for granted about where we begin and where we leave off is usually just a matter of conditioning.

As you open your heart and ask to grow, sit in that inner environment of openness for a little while and be acutely aware of the relaxation you feel as you experience that deeper state. Notice a quiet sense of well-being starting to percolate around in there. Breathe into it. As you do so, you will find that this feeling starts to expand, becoming more alive and vital. There is nothing in particular to think about, no issue to contemplate, but only this feeling of well-being to notice.

It's really an amazing thing: We have hearts in there! They are so strong and wonderful that even though we've spent years hitting them with shovels they keep bouncing back. It is simply their nature — they *will* be heard. So that is where we start. Then we discover that where we start out is where we end up. When we start from love, love is where we always find ourselves in the end.

This isn't easy all the time, but then nothing is free. If you have something wonderful in your life there is also a price to be paid for it. The real point is that whatever you nurture grows. Depression goes to depression, sadness to sadness, and love to love. When you nurture what is wonderful in your life, it has an extraordinary way of growing and taking down all the walls.

So when you are moved to look for love outside yourself, stop. Sit down and direct your attention to your heart. Focus on your heart until you feel something begin to open, and ask to grow. The more you practice doing this, the more you discover a quiet sweetness. In time, you begin to feel this sweetness expand within you as the power of all Life, which is love.

As you feel the sweetness function within you, watch how it changes your day. If it brightens your hour, that is fine; if the next hour gets brighter still, that is good, too. Look at how it changes everything. If you lose track of it, that is all right. Just stop once again and reach inside. There you will always find what you were looking for all along. Come back to this experience over and over again during the day, until you find that you are doing it naturally.

Doing this simple practice gives us a real chance to find the extraordinary beauty present in every single situation. We allow the magic inherent in that beauty to unfold its power, and to transform our whole understanding of ourselves and of the world around us.

# Taking Our Attention Inside

*I* TALK about taking our attention inside because no one needs to be told to take his or her attention to things outside. We spend a lot of our time acting like a pack of hound dogs running around in the woods with their noses to the ground, sniffing out whatever interests them. We are a serious set of sniffers. We go around sniffing out opportunities for business and relationships, along with the possibility for every kind of pleasure and pain — trying to get the one while avoiding the other.

So I rarely have to say to people, "Take your attention outside yourself and start searching for one thing or another." Focusing our attention outward is easy. (It is also, by the way, how we usually get into trouble.) On the other hand, most of us need reminding to turn our attention within. The point is to take your awareness inside and pay attention to something as simple as your heart.

Then you find that, although the technique is simple, the consequences and benefits are profound and far-reaching.

The interesting thing is that when you pay attention to the subtle sweetness of your heart and to growing as a human being, your experience of everything around you changes. For example, you find that the house could burn down, all your friends could reject you, you could be dead broke — and if your heart is open you might say, "Well, that's too bad, you know, but tomorrow is another day." You might not exactly be celebrating, but you wouldn't be destroyed, either. Instead, you would be operating from an inner strength that would enable you to go forward from there and find something of value in the experience.

Conversely you could have just inherited twenty-five million dollars and have sixteen options for marriage, and if your heart were not open you would probably be saying to yourself, "What good is all this — it's nothing." So the deeper state of your heart is a good place to start looking when you're trying to size up a situation.

Try to think about all your issues in the broadest possible context. This broad context is the awareness that the same vitality which is the power of your very soul is the same vital essence of Life that you encounter in all things. It expresses itself in you as an individual, but it is also infinite and unbounded. *You* are a part of it, just as much as *it* is a part of you.

Human experience on every level is an interplay of individual and divine, of personal and infinite. We all experience parts of ourselves that are vast and seemingly unbounded in any way. We also confront intimate, personal, and challenging physical circumstances. Moreover the personal and the infinite are interconnected in every moment. The place where the two meet is in your heart. When you know this deeply, then every idea you have ever had about who and what you are will dissolve.

You start with the experience of what is most deeply alive within you, which is what you encounter whenever you open your heart deeply and ask to grow. The alternative is to end up working from the perspective of conditioning and habit, and you already know where those things get you. So when those old records start to play the tune of the logic of survival, turn them off and start to listen instead to a deeper music — what I call the symphony of Life Itself, whose every theme and motif is the logic of love.

# The Process of Inner Work

OUR lives in the world impose pressures on us that can sometimes cause us to be less than lovers of life. If there is any real struggle in our spiritual search, it is the struggle to maintain our appreciation and love for the creative power of Life. We are challenged to maintain a degree of passion for this creative power that will allow us to transform our tensions and rise above the pressures we face. Even as our lives demand a tremendous amount of inner work, there is an underlying sense of mystery that compels us to understand the essence of our lives.

There are two ways we can fall down in our endeavor to grow as human beings. One is to become over-extended and stuck, in which case there is no more movement of our creative energy. The other is to become contracted and stuck, in which case there is also no movement. For example, when we go on the attack against somebody else and start looking for reasons to blame him or her, we become extended and locked. The other version of this is the lock in which we blame ourselves. Both of these are the inevitable outcome of trying to operate according to the logic of the ego.

Yet in growing, our objective is neither to beat up on ourselves or on anyone else. It is to develop our inner mastery as human beings and our ability to articulate that mastery in action. So every experience we have should facilitate the growth of our understanding and mastery. Then we are no longer concerned about this individual experience or that one, nor are we dragging around a load of guilt.

When approaching spiritual practices and teachings, people are sometimes concerned about what they will have to give up in order to get whatever they are pursuing. The material cost of realization is often a big concern, especially when it involves Eastern teachings and teachers. In my own tradition, as I mentioned earlier, my teacher said to me, "The only thing you have to give up is guilt. You can't close your heart to yourself or to others. *This* is your spiritual work."

Spiritual work has nothing to do with guilt or blame. It does have everything to do with deepening your awareness and understanding. This is the point of all experience. If other people try to lay blame on you, that's their problem. You don't have to accept it. You are allowed to make mistakes.

In learning about love there are many mistakes you can potentially make. But the only real mistake is to accept your own heart's closing. Sometimes you may fall down in tears over the behavior of somebody else;

sometimes you may cry over your own behavior. These two experiences are a part of growing and, ultimately, of transcending your individual limitations.

Still, no perfection is ever required of you in the endeavor to go beyond these limitations. Perfection may be the nature of love and, as you open yourself to it, that love will teach you about itself, but you are not expected to know about it ahead of time. To experience this love may break open your heart, mind, and even some of the bones in your psychological structure. That may be what it takes. But is it not better to break and grow as a person than to end your life feeling like you've missed out on what was really important about Life Itself?

The point of your inner work is to generate strength and to bring about a condition of openness in which you can begin to understand yourself differently and come to function in new ways. You work to raise yourself to the highest level of your capacity every day so that you can face life and deal with it as simply and straightforwardly as possible.

Nobody learns to do this all at once. As you unlock tensions and experience an extended flow of creative energy within yourself, that experience of flow won't just get rid of all your problems. In fact, for a long time it may seem to reveal more problems than it solves. That's all right — it's part of the process. Those problems were probably there all along, buried under layers of tension about other things.

So you will probably experience more mistakes than successes for a while. That's all right, too, as long as you don't keep on making the same mistakes over and over again. If you really want to grow, then you simply make the effort to keep letting go of your impulse to close up. You open your heart, instead, to doing things differently. That's all. The point is not to expect that you are immediately going to get a merit badge out of this process, because once anyone starts to deal with their issues, *that's* when they find out just how much there is to clean up. You just do what you can do, a day at a time.

There is also no point in crying over the amount of work in front of us. Better just to button up our guts and get to work. The problem with crying over it is that this is often what we've already spent a lot of time doing, and look where we've ended up!

In doing all this work, the stillness and sweetness you discover within your own heart become the point of reference from which you can genuinely function in the world. In the process, you will have to confront your desires, attachments, and tensions. At the same time, you will have the opportunity to dissolve these things if you choose. You can dissolve them in a way that ends up expanding the love, respect, and devotion you feel for Life Itself. You become a bigger person.

In that broader awareness, you can more easily discriminate between what is truth and what is not. You find that much of your experience is just noise — not necessarily false, but noise nevertheless. The remainder is truth, and it is important to attend to it. Understanding this, you don't have to invest so much energy in the noise. Moreover when you take your energy out of the noise, then all the patterns of tension, strain, and disturbance related to it just melt away.

They melt away because you consciously choose to do things differently from the way you have done them before. You choose to act from a different starting point and to implement a different logic in your life. When you encounter tensions, instead of acting them out you can think to yourself, "If I care about being a loving, respectful, devoted person seeking to promote everybody's highest best interest in this situation (including my own) then how do I behave?" You can ask yourself this question and think about it. In fact, this is a skill you can perfect.

Perfecting this skill is essential to your capacity to enter into a new level of rapport. In that rapport there is no "other" with whom to be in tension. Instead there is only love, respect, and devotion. This love, respect, and devotion operate not for any *purpose*, but simply as the essential, dynamic quality that *is* Life.

# The Love We Seek

So THE logic of love is that we are not here to get something, but to give something. In giving, we discover and unfold a remarkable wealth from within ourselves, like an oasis emerging in a desert. An oasis provides something simple and life-sustaining just by being there. It doesn't chase anybody; it's not trying to dump its water on anyone. It is just there, giving life and needing nothing in return. Yet around oases in the desert, great cities emerge. The point is to be like that — to give in that spirit. Then, Life Itself gives us everything.

Learning to give does not happen without some hardship. If we expect to *get* something through the process of opening our hearts, asking to grow, and living genuinely from love every day — if we expect to avoid having our hearts shattered and replaced six times, our intestines torn out and walked on, and our heads broken over and over again, we are mistaken. Living hurts. This is just one of the by-products of existing. Sometimes it is seriously hard work. If we mind that, we might as well give up now.

In the bigger picture, though, whether we open our hearts or not, whether we live with love or not, we are still going to get hurt every single day. This is true whether we live with love, or with total animosity, cynicism, and greed. So we have to decide how we want to do it. Do we want to live a happy life or a miserable one? However we choose, there will be pain involved. There is pain in living, pain in loving, and pain in growing; there is no getting around it. But the pain becomes something wonderful when we understand its tremendous power to uplift us. This happens when we learn to let go and stay open to Life Itself.

When we understand that we are not in this life to *get* but to *give*, then we are no longer playing what I call the game of life. The difference between the two positions is a basic change of attitude that reflects itself in a willingness to work at remaining open and in a deepening commitment to growing as human beings. When we no longer expect to be repaid for everything we do and our whole focus is no longer on our own wishes or our own comfort, then the whole game changes. When we understand that we are here to give something and not to get anything in particular, then everything we do becomes a participation in this infinitely creative display we call Life Itself.

This simple difference in attitude brings about a profoundly different kind of experience. As long as we are looking for easy ways to *get*, we go on playing the game.

But when we understand that we are here to give, then everything we do becomes an opportunity to further pursue what we love. Everything becomes something we can share with people as part of the creative work we are developing within ourselves. While this may not get us ahead in a material sense, it is a wide open opportunity to further unfold our understanding of ourselves and to deepen the quality of our lives. Ultimately, this understanding is the only thing we possess, and the one thing no one can take away from us.

In order to get love we have to give it first. Moreover love is not a business exchange. We empty ourselves in order to be renewed, not to be paid back. By spending and extending ourselves, we discover more of our own fullness.

When we say, "I can't give very much," or "I have only so much to give," we are actually short-changing ourselves. It doesn't matter whether what we give is tiny or big, because in the process of giving and paying attention to the source within ourselves from which we give, we enter into something infinite. There, distinctions like big and small, left and right, up and down, or coming and going have no meaning.

Every single means by which we learn to open our hearts is like a tool we use to break the lock and open the door so that love can start to flow inside and around us. If we don't get distracted by keeping accounts — if we don't keep checking to be sure we're getting something for each thing we're giving — then slowly this love increases. It unfolds and shows itself for all that it is. Then it's the love that is teaching us, even as it endlessly reveals itself to be our own essence. This is both serious, and completely light and joyous, all at the same moment.

All techniques and tools work like that. We can use them for a hundred thousand years and get nowhere, as long as we are trying to keep score. It is really one moment of looking love dead in the eye that takes us everywhere in a flash.

If we find ourselves saying, "I'm giving love, but I'm not getting any back," we might consider that whatever we get back wears the face of what we have really given. Then we should think about what we are giving. We might also consider the possibility that we don't yet know what real love is.

My own feeling is that everyone knows in their hearts what love is *not*, and that when we see real love, we recognize it. When we look within our own hearts, we will always find the love we seek. Then whenever we have some worry or problem, we give it over to that love. We just hand it over. If we have some fear, love will guard us. If we have a journey to make, love will lead us. There is no place we can be where love is not.

# Rapport

*Our experience of rapport should take us beyond our ordinary experience of wants and needs, so that we are in a  position to start discovering the vastness of the love within  us — a vastness which will carry us beyond every limitation into a condition of inner stillness.*

# Centering

$A$s you learn about love, you will discover that your focus must be two-fold: First, you learn to establish a rapport within yourself. This includes your heart, mind, and body — in other words, your whole internal flow of creative energy. Second, you extend this awareness of yourself into your rapport with others. In this way, you cultivate a harmonious connection with all the fields of your experience.

Rapport requires that we train ourselves to be centered — not just on Wednesdays and Fridays of the odd months, but most of the time. When we cannot manage to do *that*, we at least learn to stay quiet until we can. As our creative energy reorganizes itself and we find all kinds of things changing within us, it is sometimes difficult to achieve clarity. I am one hundred percent sympathetic to this. But when something is not clear, the best policy is to keep our mouths shut and not to *do* anything. We don't decide anything and we don't take any big steps about which we cannot be clear. We don't have to engage in life-changing decisions in a state of confusion.

The way to resolve the confusion and recover a sense of rapport with yourself is very simple. If you are confronted by difficult circumstances, you can sit down, open your heart, ask to grow, and get a little bit quieter and a little more still. Then, maybe some clarity can come into the picture. This is definitely possible.

You are the only one who can do your own inner work. This work is what allows you to find and sustain your own center. Otherwise, it is all too easy to try and set up a center in someone or something else. But with your own center in place, you can absorb these other experiences and keep your balance at the same time. The whole issue is one of working to keep yourself on track.

In the experience of rapport with others, it is sometimes difficult to stay in your own center. The key is to sustain a rapport with yourself and with your own potential for transforming the quality of your life. That is the basis for a rapport with anyone else.

One of the things you can do to establish a rapport with yourself on a regular, moment-to-moment basis is the practice of centering. This is simple, yet the implications of doing it are big. For example, the most basic way of finding your center is to go through your day being aware of your breathing. You also practice opening your heart and asking to grow. Simple things like this can change everything in your awareness profoundly.

We can talk about what happens as a kind of remembering or mindfulness, but it is not exactly that, either.

Rather it is the beginning of your ability to develop a rapport with yourself and your environment, and then to sustain that rapport. You become aware of the tensions in yourself and the imbalances between you and your environment, and you address them. This is the building of rapport.

What insures this rapport over the long term is that you consciously cultivate it every day of your life. That is why we say we are living a spiritual *life*, instead of having a spiritual *moment*. When you lose touch with that rapport, you simply pick yourself up and get back to work. You have to keep working to find your center and stay there. That's all it is — staying on center and not letting yourself get knocked off it. It is just work. There is no magic button, and success at it comes from doing the work. Like everything else, mastery evolves from practice.

The more we go along, the more we recognize that the vision we have of our own lives is immaterial and flawed. It is generally based on our biological impera- tives to eat and reproduce — and most of our activities end up being one form or another of these concerns. But when we can go beyond what we have imagined for our lives, we discover that our lives have a vision for *us* to which we can connect on a regular basis. This is true Self-discovery.

Moreover, we find that the things we do to get what we want rarely get us where we really wanted to go. The external circumstances we establish do not usually bring about the quality of experience we hoped they would. We enter a situation with hope and, much of the time, find that this hope itself was an illusion. The same is true of the fear with which we go into something, because hope and fear are two sides of the same coin.

What matters throughout all these experiences is that, through our internal rapport with ourselves, we connect to our own internal state. We do so in a way that allows the changes in our lives to permeate us in the deepest way possible. This is where skillful means are required, along with our ability to connect with the people around us. We work to rise above our tensions in order to articulate the experience of our center through our whole environment.

This is a process of discovery. A deeper life within us is trying to articulate itself, so we keep still in order to become attuned to it. When we are attuned to our egos and desires, we are not attuned to our potential for change. Rather we are only acting out our illusions and can't really learn anything. This is because all illusions are self-reinforcing, self-defensive routines that only fortify our egos.

Opening our hearts and finding our center, confronting our own tensions, and taking a counter-intuitive approach to our responses allows us to turn around and face whatever we fear. It also enables us to examine what we want with a little more discretion, so that we are not so busy running from some things and chasing others. Being centered, we begin to deal with everything that comes our way in an open and honest manner.

Without this practice, we will not mature in our inner work or develop the discrimination necessary to distinguish between a narrow sense of self and the deepest Self that we really are. So the point of our inner work is to establish a rapport within ourselves, in order to have access to the flow of creative energy within us. Having gotten access to that flow, we extend it into the broader field of our lives. Doing this is what will teach us more and more about the Self.

# Giving You Yourself

$R$ EAL rapport should give you yourself. "Giving you yourself" means that you become a person who is integrated as a human being — whose cylinders are all working. It means that your brain works, you are alert and can function, and you have feelings that you can sort out. You are thoughtful, you can anticipate the future consequences of your present actions, and you can modify your behavior accordingly. "Giving you yourself" also means recognizing that certain aspects of your life are just the way they are. While they may not seem wonderful, they are nevertheless all right.

The amazing thing is that having acquired yourself, you are lifted out of a smaller understanding of yourself to discover that there is an extraordinary power available to you. This power has nothing to do with the individual self in any way, but is the power of love — the power of the Self which is alive in all things. When you discover that love within yourself, it raises you above both your pluses and minuses. Even your limitations don't seem to obstruct you in the same way. Then you interact with everyone around you differently, and have relationships of a very different kind, in which Self is relating to Self.

Our relationships are really only meaningful in direct proportion to the depth of our rapport with the Self within us. If we don't have that rapport, then every other one of our relationships is in some way superficial. This has everything to do with the nature of the love in our own hearts. There is an old Indian saying that we see the world the way we are. If this is so, then it is necessary to keep our attention in our own hearts, concentrate on feeling the love within ourselves, and be as authentic as we can with everybody else.

In this process, we should pretty much forget about worrying whether or not other people are nice to *us*. In growing, we are genuinely concerned about one thing, and that is both knowing and articulating the love in our own hearts. This has to be our real concern and not "What am I going to get out of this?" We want to learn what it means to be a clear-headed, stand-up person who is, at the same time, capable of loving deeply. We do this by first learning to be friends with ourselves.

Otherwise, it is not so easy to be a loving person. After all, almost everybody would like to be a loving person, yet very often we are not. What happens is that when we start to get a little bit agitated or threat-ened, our lovingness can evaporate in a flash. This is ironic, because it is just at such moments that we need it the most.

I don't ever want to *assume* I am a loving person. If I do that, then I may begin to act in ways that don't really have anything to do with the authenticity or living quality of the given moment. Moreover, I have seen lots of people who assume they are loving, yet who have done some terrible things to other people — even as they cling vigorously to the idea of being loving. Whole crusades and inquisitions have gotten started that way. So we don't want this to become our assumption, because it is too easy for it to become part of our personal propaganda — that is, the message we give ourselves and others about who and what we are.

Instead both the discovery of the love within us and our effort to be loving people should constitute our inner practice and become the basis by which we live our lives. We become friends with ourselves by first learning to open our hearts. When we practice doing this, what we find there teaches us the way to become steady in each circumstance. That steadiness brings a new depth into every moment.

Then a wonderful thing happens. When we bring in this new depth, we find a vitality, a brightness, even a brilliance that shines forth from us because we are open. We see ideas, insights, and action flow forth from us, and the power of inspiration can function within us, transforming us and our environment.

We are continuously searching for and participating in that inspiration. Over time we explore its power and vitality. Knowing the vitality of that inspiration is the essence of any spiritual life. So I would say that we aim not to search for love in the world or from others. We search, instead, for love within ourselves and seek to live lives inspired by that love.

# Service

$T$HE point of opening your heart and centering yourself over and over again is to bring about a fusion in your awareness of what is inner and what is outer. The expression of this fusion occurs as an attitude of service. I am using the term "service" to refer both to a transformation within yourself — insofar as this process serves *you* — and to a transformation in the circumstances of your life. This, too, is an attitude of service. When you serve, you are not merely serving another individual; you are serving everything at once, both internal and external.

Finding your center and cultivating an attitude of service should ultimately lead you to being able to serve others in ways they may not be aware of needing to be served. I say this because the most refined form of service happens when we serve the potential within others which they may not even know they have.

Let me give a simple analogy from manufacturing: The development of a product often happens in response to a perceived need. This level of production does not necessarily have anything to do with a concern for quality. A second level of production involves the effort to make the very best of whatever is being produced, so that *it* becomes the standard of excellence. This is a second level of service. But the highest level of service involves making the thing so creatively and well that it satisfies needs people didn't even know they had. In the hierarchy of attaining quality, the highest level is the fulfillment of unconscious needs.

As you learn to transform your own tensions and to contain your own agendas, the important thing is to start to see into the depth of other people. You are able to manage yourself and participate in your relationships in ways that really serve the long-term interests of others — perhaps in ways that their individual awareness has not allowed them to recognize.

This is a tricky thing. In every case, one test of whether you are on the mark or not will be the response of the other person. If your service is real, he or she will experience it as the turning on of a light, as the revelation of something brilliant, or as a relief in his or her own field of function. This test is important, because otherwise you are likely to start trying to convince others that you are doing something necessary that they just don't know about — which may only end up being a rationalization for manipulating the situation.

You can tell the difference in two ways. First, when you are centered, deeply quiet within yourself, and relating to your whole life with an attitude of quiet, then opportunities for doing things simply happen.

The second thing is to ask yourself the question: Is this really serving both of us, or just me? If you can't be really sure it is serving the best interest of everyone involved, then it is better not to do it. If the event is real, it will certainly come around again — whatever is needed will remain. It is only when something is an illusion that it disappears.

I raise these issues to suggest the depth of potential for knowing ourselves and for serving our total environment. This potential is not something we have to make happen, because if we achieve a real depth of openness and surrender within ourselves, then this dimension within us simply starts to function. The point is simply to be aware of it, because it helps us to recognize that the deepest, real needs exist beyond the reaches of the mind. They are revealed not in thinking or feeling, or in our desires, ambitions, hopes, or fears. Rather they reveal themselves of their own accord and by their own power, in moments of simple openness and stillness.

# The Highest Best Interest

$I$N THE process of setting up a rapport both with ourselves and others, we will definitely confront our egos. So if we are going to deepen that rapport, we are going to have to become a lot more skillful about how we express ourselves — a lot more observant about the feelings we embrace within ourselves as well as the feelings we don't embrace. We will have to train ourselves to think, "What is my own highest best interest in this situation, what is the highest best interest of everybody else, and how do I connect to, express, and support that highest best interest?"

If we don't learn to ask ourselves this question, then in one way or another we are falling back into the self-perpetuating, self-reinforcing patterns of egotism. So to think in a progressive way that takes us beyond our own selfish needs is essential. This we do by making the *choice* to do so. Otherwise how do we get out of a narrow view of things? It is very difficult.

In the process we will have to confront our own greed, selfishness, insecurity, arrogance, stupidity, and so forth. This isn't much fun. But it does provide us with the raw material for tremendous change. If we can take this raw material and genuinely transform ourselves as a result, then our horizons become unlimited.

Unlimited horizons emerge from our ability to establish and sustain a profound rapport within ourselves. Then we find ourselves more and more in rapport with Life Itself. This rapport is subtle. It won't hit us over the head; it is simply there, in the same way the essence of Life Itself is always there. It has no need to announce its presence; it just *is*. The issue is our awareness of it.

Our experience of rapport should take us beyond our ordinary experience of our individual wants and needs, so that we are in a position to start discovering the vastness of the love that always exists within us — a vastness which will carry us beyond every limitation of our bodies and minds, beyond every life issue, into a condition of inner stillness. In that condition of stillness, we encounter a rapport which is so immediate and complete that we can state unequivocally that all of Life is only one, not many.

As long as we perceive even *one* "other," then we are in the same situation. The perception of two easily becomes the perception of ten thousand. As long as we perceive two, we experience some sense of tension. Whether immediately and in a flash, or gradually over time, we hope to participate in that rapport to a degree that we awaken to the fact that there are not two functioning here, but only one. That *one* is not any individual, but the dynamic power of Life Itself.

Then we move from the experience of "other" to one of a flow of energy and of connection. This eventually brings us to the experience of union, in which there is only one. This union is the real object of every spiritual endeavor. It is union with Life Itself — with the essence of everything that is.

Real rapport does not annihilate us. We are not interested in being annihilated or in somehow losing ourselves in the person of any other. This is not what rapport is about. As I said earlier, rapport is about gaining ourselves — gaining the experience and direct contact with another that allows us to recognize that the energetic essence of the many is actually one thing.

We want to gain and realize our own deepest Self. That is the point of inner mastery. When we live our lives fully understanding who we really are, we then live out a rapport not only with ourselves, but with Life Itself. That is freedom; that is liberation. It is also what is sometimes called salvation. It is what shows us that Life is really one.

This experience doesn't necessarily make our lives materially abundant, nor does it necessarily put an end to our loneliness. It does, however, give us an understanding of what these things are all about, and of how unimportant they are relative to the power of Life Itself within and around us. So it is not that all the little issues in life go away. Instead we recognize how profoundly insignificant they are in the context of the vastness and power of Life Itself, a power which is always accessible to us if we turn our attention to it. It is our experience of that power that teaches us about authentic love.

# Honesty

IN ESTABLISHING rapport with ourselves and others, two things are fundamentally important: First, we must be honest with ourselves, and second, we must do no harm. Some people would also say that this should include being honest with others. This, however, is trickier than it sounds.

When we don't know a person well, we are more likely to sustain a certain level of courtesy and to be careful about what we say. When we get comfortable and when a certain rapport is established — especially in our close relationships — then a change can take place. My teacher Rudi used to quote the old saying, "Familiarity breeds contempt." In a way, as we become familiar with the other person, we are also more likely to become disrespectful. We get comfortable enough to say whatever is on our minds, and think that this is the kind of honesty and truth to which we should aspire. We stop thinking about the real value we are trying to communicate.

This is not a good thing either for us or for the relationship, because it doesn't express real respect or value for anybody. So we have to cultivate our respect for other people by thinking carefully about what we are trying to say, and saying only those things that will promote the relationship. By this I mean what will further the highest best interest of all concerned.

First we have to know what we want to say. Then we have to say it simply and in a way that can be heard. If we have to choose between being more loving and less honest, then I would go so far as to say it is better to be loving. This may sound like hypocrisy or avoidance, but it's not.

Why? Because a lot of times what we think of as honesty is not. Let me put it this way: You can be honest with me and tell me what you *really* feel, and in fifteen minutes — or two weeks — be feeling something completely different. In the process, the "honesty" of the moment ends up polluting the environment of our relationship and takes all kinds of time to clean up.

First and foremost, we should be honest about the love, and take the time to sift through our feelings. Often the feelings that set themselves up in us are really reflections of whatever is going on within or around us, and are neither tangible nor clear. We change that lack of clarity not by setting it out there for someone else to stumble over, but by working to bring a greater openness to the moment. Then whatever is really happening can come to the surface. After that we will see it manifest through our behavior in ways that we can actually talk about.

It is better to limit our honesty to discussions of pragmatic issues concerning behavior: In a clear and simple way, we can ask that certain things be done differently. In making such requests we don't have to tell our whole life story; we just ask. This is quite different from telling someone what we think of them and of their behavior. In the latter kind of conversation, we get caught up in the more temporary aspects of our experience. Our feelings change a lot, and fifteen minutes of honesty can destroy what it took us years to put together.

All of us have times when we are not exactly wild about ourselves or our lives. Sometimes we feel jammed up and closed. But just because we feel this way, we can't succumb to the temptation to beat up on the people around us or accuse them of one thing or another. If we feel tense, tight, or uncertain, rather than being "honest" with somebody else it is better to open ourselves and let the goodness within us function.

This is especially important if we want to have a long-term relationship with somebody. If our zeal for honesty and directness creates tensions, then those tensions will build up in the relationship, distort the whole process of communication, and undermine our rapport with someone else. We have to understand from the start that every time we fight with somebody we leave a trace of tension — some filter through which each succeeding communication will pass and strain out the rapport.

As much as possible we don't want to set up this filter. So there has to be a give and take based not on total self-denial but on the understanding that everybody has real needs that have to be met. We want to meet those real needs in ways that create as little tension and crystallization as possible, so that over time we still have a vital, loving relationship.

The only other thing I would add to this is that if we haven't got a sense of humor about ourselves and everything else, we're in deep trouble.

# Practice

*A*UTHENTIC love is an experience that requires tremendous patience, persistence, and an incredible amount of surrender. Beyond that, it takes the ability to pick ourselves up every single day and release whatever disappointments we have encountered. A disappointment is an occasion in which a flow simply isn't happening, and which there is no point in pursuing.

When we find ourselves disappointed, we have to learn when to drop something and get on with our lives. We also have to be able to shift gears relatively rapidly, even as we maintain a high degree of enthusiasm. That shouldn't be too hard, because if we are really connected in rapport, it's a wonderful thing. We can easily feel enthusiastic about Life just from that. We just have to work to stay open, flowing, and observant of this rapport.

So have value for the rapport in your life and take it seriously. When you wake up in the morning, be about setting up that rapport within yourself. As you move through your day, take every opportunity to establish and extend the rapport you have with yourself and your environment.

The latter is a little tougher, initially, because your environment will give you a lot of feedback, some of which you may not like. If you can remain open to it, however, ultimately you become a subtle and sophisticated person — able to maintain your awareness of the flow of creative energy and the interconnectedness of all living things, even as you move about in the world of diversity. Your experience of the distinctions between what is internal and external will be enormously diminished, and you will find endless opportunities in your everyday life to experience an expansion of spirit and a deepening of rapport on every level.

Rapport does not happen by accident, but as the result of continuous, conscious effort. It comes out of the effort you make to rise above your tensions, desires, ambitions, and struggles to get in touch with this deeper harmony. It is the inner work you do to act out that harmony in the context of whatever your life gives you to do.

Rapport is a little bit like performing music, in this sense: It is both a discipline in practice, and a release at the same time. It is initially a way of directing your energy, and becomes the vehicle through which a release happens and a potentially marvelous expression takes place. It may not always feel wonderful or even special, but it is always rewarding and regularly extraordinary.

This condition of rapport is worthy of great value and respect. When we are striving for it and learning to open ourselves more deeply to it, we can expect to experience disturbances. This is not so surprising, because we are reorganizing our fundamental ways of interacting not only with ourselves but with everything around us. The disruption in our customary patterns of behavior can be a little bit disturbing. My teacher Rudi's attitude in this regard was quite clear. He felt that we ourselves are responsible not only for the disturbance but also for alleviating it.

If we are to alleviate it, we have to practice being flexible and open. Whatever the agenda we have cooking, once we recognize it to be an obstruction to the flow of the rapport, we have to be prepared to drop it in a flash. This is so, regardless of the changes it requires of us.

Whenever we have some agenda at work — especially if it has been around for a while before we recognize it as a problem — it is going to carry with it all kinds of subsidiary issues. All of these issues are related to the question, "What's going to happen to me?" This is because in the context of an evolving rapport, every kind of egotistical issue will present itself. But the real answer to the ego's question here is, "It doesn't really matter."

What *does* matter is that the rapport be sustained and that, in a deeper and deeper way, we allow authentic love to inform our attitudes and behavior. If we care about being good people and about growing as human beings, then our basic inner work is about generating an environment of love within ourselves so that our hearts remain open and our minds stay clear under all kinds of pressure, so we can be thoughtful about how to manifest this love.

Love is not just a matter of words. Lots of people say, "I love you" without really manifesting love in their lives. Love is not what we *say;* it is what we *do.* So when we observe that things are not working out for us with the people we say we love, then we have to pull back and try to see where our own behavior may be falling short. We have to think about what real love would look like in those moments, and be thoughtful about it. In fact, it is perfectly fine to contemplate this issue deeply, so that we end up legitimately and authentically changing our behavior.

The rapport you cultivate is the context in which you allow love to inform every aspect of your existence. Such love emerges, first, from the rapport you have within yourself. It also has to manifest in the rapport you have with the whole field of your life, including everyone who lives in that field. That's where it gets real. The reality of your love is tested in the field of your life, and is also fed back to you through your interactions with others. It is through this testing process that you come to know the practical meaning and the tremendous power of this love.

# The Symphony of Life

*A* SPIRITUAL life is the process of cultivating our contact with what I call the symphony of Life within us — something that we literally feel inside ourselves every day. We train ourselves to attune our minds to it and we go on to feel it as we move through our day. That's what a spiritual life is.

This contact makes every single person with whom we interact somehow special; it makes every moment of encounter significant. This doesn't mean every time we sit around talking about baseball that the conversation itself is significant. That is not the point. The point is that we become aware enough within ourselves that we experience the rapport between ourselves and others even if we are talking gibberish.

In my interactions with others I assume that up to ninety-nine percent of the verbal interaction may be essentially surface noise, and I don't take it all that seriously. The remaining one percent, however, is significant information. That part I take seriously, allowing everything else to come and go.

Yet on a deeper level I would also say that the experience of rapport makes every moment significant. Every moment presents an opportunity to extend our contact with the essence of Life, and to move with total concert and harmony in the field of our own lives. This is a wonderful thing.

In the stillness we discover within our hearts, we first hear the symphony of Life. This is not a personal symphony — it is not about me or you as individuals. Rather it is universal, because it is the Life in all things. It is simply there, *being* itself. There is nothing to be done with it. It is a lot smarter than we are and knows quite a bit more about its own function than we do. So we practice opening our hearts, being still within ourselves, and becoming attuned to the inner stillness of the symphony. In that openness and surrender, the stillness we experience is what teaches us to move in harmony with the flow of our lives, never losing sight of what our lives are about. In this way we grow as human beings.

I spoke earlier about service. Ideally we want to find an internal integration. We want to develop an understanding of the appropriate distance between ourselves and other people in order to develop a sense of appropriate service. It is a wonderful thing to think that total selflessness is our objective, but this is not entirely true. It may be required at points in our life, but we have to find an appropriate balance in which we benefit, others benefit, and there is a real give-and-take. There are times when we give, and times when the other person gives. It is not good to keep score, but it is good to be observant.

So our fundamental attitude and commitment must be one of service. This orientation grows out of our basic inner experience of rapport and love. In fact if that love is going to inform our whole life, and if we are going to be people acting out authentic love instead of people just talking love for greedy reasons, then we have to find that rapport and make a daily effort to be in touch with it. We have to learn to feel it in our hearts and let that feeling inform our thoughts and actions.

It is something like listening to music. If we listen to a rock-and-roll record that we really like, it creates a certain feeling in us. The same is true of a classical piece. Each kind of music creates a set of feelings. As we get in touch with those feelings, they start to inform our bodies. We may feel like dancing, certain kinds of thoughts occur in our minds, and other feelings flow from the   first one.

In attuning ourselves to the resonance of a rapport, we are simply learning to dance the dance of divine life. We are learning to participate completely in its symphony. Then rapport is our total attunement to the cosmic musician, whose notes condense to form the manifestation of the whole world.

The music of Life Itself is what I refer to as love. This music is ever present and always available to us in our experience of rapport. We deny ourselves access to it when our creative energy contracts into the tensions in which we get caught up and which we sustain. These tensions set up a vibration that doesn't allow us to become subtle or quiet enough to participate in that inner rapport. This is why opening our hearts and transforming our tensions back into creative energy is important to our ability to grow and to experience the love within us. Tension cannot support the kind of integration that emerges from the experience of rapport.

This condition of rapport is what informs us about the direction, nature, and quality of any act of service we hope to perform. As we cultivate this rapport, opportunities for serving simply arise in a way that shows us how they are to be carried out. The details can easily be known through our subtle contact with that state within us. It is when we are trying to *think* about it or have some agenda of our own mixed up with it that we can never really connect to the deeper reality.

Interestingly, we might be able to do an acceptable job. We might see an opportunity to serve and fulfill it from a condition of some kind of egotism. The difficulty, however, is that we will never do it completely or, in a way, brilliantly, because true virtuosity and genius really emerge from a condition of rapport.

Why do I say this? Because in a condition of rapport, we discover experientially that all the apparently diverse elements of any action or creative endeavor are really one thing. They are all expressions of the creative energy of Life Itself. When we see how everything is connected, we recognize the appropriate way to approach any particular occasion. Such an approach is the one that facilitates the simple, natural unfolding of a balance and harmony that is brilliant, beautiful, and extraordinary. This is the fulfillment of rapport.

# Transforming Tension

*Our inner work involves letting go of our identification with our tension and opening our hearts instead. In the process, we discover our capacity to transcend our limitations, transform our lives, and know the essence of our lives from the core of our own souls.*

# Inner Work

*I*T IS fascinating to see people work out their tensions with one another in relationships. Most of the hurt that goes back and forth between us is not really about "me hurting you" or "you hurting me." It only looks that way. Actually it is the struggle that each of us goes through to work out our own tensions. This is because each of our tensions represents a place where we find it difficult to be open to somebody else. That difficulty is directly related to the ego and its preoccupation with what will happen to us if we *do* open ourselves.

So we want to attend to that struggle directly and not take it out on other people. That's all. Otherwise our various struggles become just another excuse for living with our hearts closed. If we're not careful, that state of closedness becomes a whole environment we set up around us that attracts more tension from within itself and thereby only reinforces itself over and over again.

When we are closed, everything we see around us becomes simply another reason to be closed. Everybody looks like some kind of a so-and-so, which seems like further proof that we should keep our hearts closed to them, and everything we encounter seems like just another piece of bad news — and so there we are, once again reinforcing the tension, the tightness, and the whole sense of struggle we have with the world. "I've got to get them before they get me." How much fun is it to live that way?

Yet when we open our hearts and do the inner work every day to be open — and it does require an effort every day to remain open — we start to see something special in ourselves. That "special" pulls what is special out of other people. Slowly, we see "special" everywhere and our lives become qualitatively different. The tensions that come to us, the challenges we face, and whatever closedness we encounter become just something else to which we open ourselves.

Anything short of continuously working to attain this genuine openness and love in our lives ultimately becomes an acceptance of the opposite. If we persist in doing our inner work, however, where do we end up? We end up rising above all of the tensions. This is surrender. It is also inner mastery. In the process, two things happen. One is that we genuinely discover love. At the same time, we become much bigger people from the experience.

It is all too easy and all too convenient not to do our inner work. We get to a point where we feel like giving up and saying, "Oh, I tried. I really tried but I just couldn't do it." What kind of rationalization is that? Either we are doing our inner work or we are setting up a justification. It is that simple.

It is easy to make excuses for ourselves, but all that does is shift the whole reason for our tensions onto others. Then what kind of personal responsibility are we taking for our lives? We have to do our own inner work. Sometimes that means we just sit there and work to open inside. Whenever we find ourselves in a contracted state, we sit there and basically do what all the great sages throughout history have done: We bust our guts. We sit there, we ask to grow, and we churn and burn inside as we work to open ourselves and transform the tension. In fact, we do whatever we have to until the tension finally releases.

This is not the same thing as getting tight and intense. This is the paradox. What our inner work involves is letting go of our identification with our tension, and opening our hearts instead. In the process, we discover our capacity to transcend our limitations, transform our lives, and know the essence of our lives from the core of our own souls. This is our inner work.

The inner work of transforming tensions is a two-part skill. One part involves your inner effort. This means learning to stay relaxed, keep an open mind, and be non-judgmental. In other words, it is the effort to keep your heart open, to sustain a creative flow within yourself, and to practice letting go every day. The other part involves the skill necessary to extend this inner openness into the flow with another person or situation.

I make these distinctions for the purpose of discussion. In practice, they cannot exactly be separated. The point is that you train yourself to stay open on the one hand, and focused on growing as a human being on the other. Then whether you meet up with tension within yourself or encounter it in somebody else, you are not thrown off balance.

All tension is nothing but strong energy. We can, of course, always react to the strong energy of another person's tension by closing up within ourselves or by becoming emotional and spewing it back out all over the place. In doing so, however, we only feed the original misunderstanding that caused the gap in the first place. In fact, whenever we react, we usually make things worse.

The alternative is the counter-intuitive approach of taking a step back, learning to connect to that strong energy, and staying open in the midst of it. When we can do this, we also stay open to the flow of creative energy within ourselves. Then we allow the strong energy of the tension to flow within us, even as we flow within it. In the process, we transform it from tension into creative energy, which is what it really started out being in the first place. The more we do this, the more we recognize that what we are really dealing with is the creative energy of Life Itself.

Because we learn to be thoughtful and careful in moments of tension, we discover something important about ourselves, about the situation to which we're relating, and about other people. We find that we can allow the creative content of a situation to unfold itself, free of any willful limitation we might place upon it. Then as this creative energy of Life Itself unfolds and articulates its own inner content, we ourselves are uplifted along with everyone involved. This is an incredible learning process and an extraordinary gift.

# Investing in Our Lives

$I$N EVERY kind of relationship there come points where
tensions arise that will challenge your ability to open
yourself more deeply. Still for the sake of your own life
you cannot allow your heart to close. It is *your* heart, and
it deserves to be open.

It doesn't matter what kind of low-life, mean, and
rotten people have been a part of your life. For that
matter, there are a lot of them out there in the world —
maybe more than any other single category. Some people
are only out for themselves and don't know any better.
They use and hurt other people, they constantly create
tensions around themselves, and they have no ability to
do anything else well. However for you to become closed
as a result only diminishes *you* and narrows your own life.

This is true for all of us. To respond by trying to be
out for ourselves in any way is a bad strategy, because in

the long run it uses up the resources of good will, respect, and care that exist in our environment, and leaves us with a shell of a life. I see many people who had every opportunity to do something wonderful with their lives, but because they were only out for themselves, everybody around them eventually got sick of dealing with them. They ended up with no credibility, and therefore no respect.

Credibility and respect are important, even among criminals. We have to value them ourselves, so that as we go along we build them up in our own lives. They will then serve as resources — as a richness within and around us that will give us some room to move, create, think, feel, and express ourselves. They give us real avenues in many areas of our lives, so that we end up with a life and not a prison.

If we think of life as more than the six weeks or so that lie ahead of us, we understand that five and ten years from now we are still going to be around and doing. So it becomes important for us to look beyond the tensions of the moment and invest ourselves in the people in our lives in a thoughtful way. Moreover when I say "thoughtful," I am not talking about the return we expect to get. We don't make this investment because of some expectation about what we are going to get back from anyone. That is only to play back into the logic of survival.

If we think in terms of what we expect in return, to what does that lead? Well, if I do something for you with the expectation that you are going to pay me back, that's not love — that's a business deal. Moreover it's not even an investment; it's a loan. Since we usually don't feel all that good about the people to whom we owe money compared with the people who just help us out without expecting anything in return, the difference is a critical one.

Furthermore, if we invest in someone else with the idea that this gives us the right to say how things are going to be done, then we didn't invest; we bought. And how do we feel about somebody who tries to tell us what to do — especially when we're not so sure that we sold anything, while the other person is quite sure that he or she bought? To be in this situation only creates tensions and problems for everybody.

So we can't enter into our relationships as though they were loans or purchases. They must simply be investments, and not even investments we make with the expectation that they are going to perform. Rather we invest ourselves in the life we have around us, which consists of other people and, to some degree, the work we have to do. When we approach our lives in this way, there is every likelihood that our investment as a whole will grow and represent a source of energy and strength. This energy will be of tremendous benefit to us over the long haul.

For this to happen, however, we have to be thoughtful about how, and what, and in which ways we invest — not chintzy, but thoughtful. What it boils down to over and over again is our willingness to work hard and really put ourselves out. It also requires an ability to observe from which sources the deepest feedback in our lives is coming. We see what that feedback is and we refine our capacity to respond to it in a real way.

Then instead of acting like barriers through which a lot of information is filtered out and only tensions are left behind, we become events beyond barriers — events in whom the interplay of information, love, and creative energy nourishes and nurtures the deepest part of us, reorganizing us continuously so that everyone involved can love and grow.

# Eating the Tensions

*I*T IS a given that our relationship to everything and everyone is going to change, no matter what we might hope to the contrary. Those points of change are always points of friction, too. So if we really care about somebody, then we must be concerned about getting through these transition points with as little tension as possible. In the long run this allows the relationship to mature to its full potential.

From time to time any balance between people will be reorganized. As that process takes place, we will experience resistance, fear, and so on. If we identify ourselves as growing people, however — instead of by gender, work, politics, or any of the other identities available to us — then these experiences of reorganization can happen more often, more powerfully, and more deeply for everyone's growth.

All the emotional and intellectual structures — the individual identities we establish — exist to buffer us from these experiences of reorganization and to suppress them. As we remove the buffers, the depth of our experience increases. In the process, we will confront fear and anxiety. During all that, we want to maintain our own inner balance and understand that, if we do so, we will establish an equilibrium of increasingly finer and greater magnitude. This is what I call "eating tensions."

By eating tensions I do *not* mean stuffing them down. This is not about absorbing environmental negativity to the detriment of our own well-being and growth. What I do mean is that we do the inner work to transform the tension back into creative energy. We do this by opening ourselves deeply to it, taking it in, learning to relax with it and digest it, in order to recover its deeper substance as nourishment.

If we are going to live in harmony and find real love with other people, we have to learn to eat the tensions that arise. This doesn't mean that we ignore or suppress them, or that we get ulcers as a result. It doesn't mean that we continue to take abuse. It does mean that we learn to look at these circumstances from a bigger perspective, so that we can have a greater sense of our choices and of our freedom.

To find this freedom, we must first to be able to rise above identifying with all our issues. Otherwise, they become obstacles we create that block the flow. When we can step back from them and return our awareness to the real love always present within us, we can then even allow these issues to exist as part of the structure that channels the flow of our creative energy. For example, we recognize the strengths we developed in response to some of the worst events in our lives. We see how they either continue to serve our creative expression, or how they have become something we can allow to fall away. When we can do this, then even our issues become something wonderful.

# Control and Balance

O N E of the biggest tensions we have to transform
is our own effort to control the people around us. While
I think that to some degree we can control ourselves —
for example, we have a certain amount of control over
our mouths — beyond that, the effort is pretty futile.
So I would say that I'm not interested in control, but
in balance.

It's a little bit like driving a car on the highway.
There is a palpable, sensory aspect to maintaining a certain balance as you move along at various rates of speed
both in traffic and on a clear road. You feel that balance
all the time. However the minute you get a little bit out of
balance, any other forces entering into the equation are
magnified enormously in their effect. If a bus comes too
close, for example, you may not be able to react very
smoothly to it.

Whenever you get out of balance, the pressures you encounter will have a magnified effect on you over which you will have little influence. Furthermore your attempts to control the pressures in a state of disequilibrium only feed more energy into the initial imbalance instead of diminishing it.

This is not to say that there is nothing you can do. You can learn how to talk and how to relate to people. You can operate with a fundamental sense of good manners and with the intention to serve people. This is a matter of basic living.

But you can be infinitely more effective in your attempts to create balance if you have cultivated that balance within yourself. In a state of balance, you expend your resources much more efficiently and productively in your daily life, your interactions with people are simpler, and you communicate your intentions more clearly on every level. In that environment you promote trust with others and a real sense of interchange that expands everyone's sense of well-being.

This is not a question of control. Even when there are parts of our lives that we have to manage, we accomplish very little by trying to control anyone else. For one thing, the more controls we institute the more information we cause others to mask. Having grown up in a highly disciplined family, I can tell you that at around the time I turned sixteen, my parents' commitment to a certain restricted approach to life caused all the information on my end to go underground. I did what I wanted to do and didn't talk about it. I'm not proud of this; it's just what happened. Their controls did not limit the parameters of my behavior. Instead the information just went elsewhere and they were unable to catch hold of it.

Instead of pushing for control, we want to promote something else in our relationships. We want to have a positive program in place, to be aware of our objectives, and to reinforce them on a regular basis. For example, everyone — including us — makes mistakes every day. We don't put an end to mistakes by reacting against them or by trying to establish more control.

When mistakes happen, we train ourselves instead to take them in stride. Instead of being punitive, we can find out how they happened. We can look at the steps we can take to prevent them from happening again, and work to improve the situation. We can also give positive feedback where it is appropriate, because we have a larger sense of what the other person may have been trying to bring about, even if he or she was unsuccessful in doing so.

When we can let go of trying to control others in our daily lives, then we generate a dynamic atmosphere in which people want to be good to themselves and to each other. This dynamic is quite different from what happens when we try to have control over others. Besides, who among us has control even over the basic flow of our lives?

The struggle for control is essentially an egotistical endeavor: "I want this. I *want* it, and I'm going to *make* it happen." Generally speaking, people with this attitude ultimately defeat themselves. Why? Because the creative energy of Life is infinitely powerful and we, as human beings, are not all that big on our own. It is when you learn to connect to that energy and flow in it that slowly your opportunities for self-expression expand. Then you

don't need control, because Life Itself is raising you up —
you don't have to pull yourself up at all.

So letting go of control brings about two benefits.
The first is that it gives you the opportunity to discover
yourself in a deeper way. The second is that it gives you
the chance to let Life Itself raise you, and allows you to
give up all struggle — to live instead both in and from
the spirit of love.

When two spiritual people meet, there is no need for
control. For that matter, there is nothing to say. The experience of love that is present dissolves everything that
can be said. No mind or thought operates in that arena —
there is nothing but quiet. They may sit like that for a
while together until at a certain moment it becomes necessary to eat. So they get up, go to the kitchen, and make
dinner. Or they go to the field and hoe the garden. Or
they go to the woods and take down a tree for wood —
whatever they need to do. They do their work, and do it
simply and quietly. It doesn't matter how complex or
sophisticated it is; it doesn't matter how much pressure it
imposes.

This is the nature of balance.

# Uncertainty

GIVING up our attempts to control things forces us to face the reality that life is really nothing but uncertainty. This is true both from the largest perspective and from a moment-to-moment point of view. Usually we try to avoid this discovery, because it is hard to recognize just how little we can control in our lives and how precarious everything really is. When we *do* recognize it, we usually translate that recognition into some kind of tension.

Uncertainty cuts both ways. On the one hand, we don't know what's going to happen, and that is a cause for concern. On the other hand, if there were really such a thing as certainty, we would all be frozen in concrete. Life would not be *alive* at all, because there would be no choice in it and little vitality. It would be less than a dream. So the experience of uncertainty also contains the potential for living authentically and truly. It holds the spectrum of infinite potential, possibility, and freedom.

In fact, uncertainty is a part of our daily experience. We don't usually notice this, because much of human activity is aimed at papering over the experience of this uncertainty. We have many ways to keep from facing the extraordinary uncertainty that goes on underneath the surface of our lives. Still it is always there.

Learning to open our hearts and to remain open is what stabilizes us in the midst of that uncertainty. It is what allows us to keep our balance at all times. When we can transform our tensions in a way that allows us to live simply in uncertainty, then we can understand the essence of our existence. To find the stillness at the center of uncertainty is the same thing as learning to keep our hearts open, and both are the same thing as surrender.

We also have to be careful not to second-guess what is going on. For example just because something in our lives looks as though it's dying away doesn't mean there is cause for worry. Every time a tree goes dormant in the winter time, we could spend time worrying about it. "Will it come back in the spring?" In fact, most springs it *will* come back — and even if that particular tree does not, for several million years enough trees have reawakened in the spring that the process as a whole continues.

The creative power of Life within us is ever self-renewing. Simply because our individual lives and our relationships don't follow the course we expected them to doesn't mean they aren't growing or that they have lost their vitality. For the most part it is our tension and our inability to manage our own anxiety that undermine the full manifestation of Life's own creative power.

So the best thing is just to keep things simple and be as cheerful as possible. After all, why not try to be light and simple? Life is much less a search for something narrowly particular than it is the discovery of a creative essence in all its expressions. When we are not absorbed in the depths of our own anxiety and depression, we have the greatest potential for identifying our opportunities and discerning how to address them.

None of us knows what's going to happen to us in our lives. But when we are simple and steady within ourselves, the opportunity for miracles to take place and the possibility of our discovering the vitality of our own lives increases immeasurably.

# Restoring a Creative Flow

*I*F WE are busy wandering all over the world searching
for love outside ourselves and expecting somebody else
to provide it, we will never stop to open ourselves and
discover that love is with us wherever we go. So whenever we search for it in someone else — whenever we
hear ourselves saying, "I wish I had some love" — it is
our ignorance talking.

The extraordinary thing is that the love we spend
so much time seeking is inside us all the time. When
we know this and turn to look within our own hearts
instead, we free this love to function. We free it to take us
to what the thirteenth-century Sufi poet, Rumi, called the
secret sky within our hearts, and to visit us in the form of
everything we encounter. Then everything remarkable
becomes possible.

Of course the remarkable doesn't happen without
some disturbance. Whatever love you set in motion by

first becoming open will start out by clearing the table before resetting it. So you can expect that any deeper love you bring to an event will cause some shifting around both within you and in the people around you. One way you discover the real values of the people in your life is by seeing how they respond to the love you bring to the situation. You don't have to make any kind of big deal about it or even discuss it very much; you just have to observe.

No matter how others respond, there is nothing anyone can do that can constitute a reason big enough to make you forfeit love. This being so, why tangle yourself up in tensions? If you are constantly fearful and worrying, tense and struggling, then you are finished.

Tensions will always naturally arise and you will deal with them as they do, but why not let your life be about the pursuit of what is truly precious? Why not allow yourself to discover the extraordinary power of love inherent in your life? Instead of always trying to mold everything and everyone around you into your own image, just love and respect them as they are and see in what ways Life Itself will shape them. This means working to stay open, no matter what.

The greatest way to articulate the love you discover within yourself is to take the tension of others and eat it. What is love, really? It is just that — taking somebody's tension, eating it, and restoring a creative flow to the situation. This means *doing* for people in a very real way, and the most real way of all is to respond to their tension by staying open to it, absorbing it, digesting it, and transforming it.

Sometimes we can't take all of it. Sometimes the person has to do something him- or herself. But if we can take even a little bit, then the person will feel the underlying dynamic of the event. That dynamic allows for movement within the person, who can then begin to process the whole mass. When we take some of that tension and eat it ourselves, we create some room for the other person to become unstuck.

On the other hand, if we try to help by giving advice, all we are doing is taking a stuck situation and trying to jam in something more: "Let's see if we can't get some more tension packed in there." Giving advice has nothing to do with loving or serving anybody. If somebody comes to us with a problem, it is a better strategy to stay open in the midst of all the tension and to keep our balance, even if we have to work hard within ourselves to do it. No matter how much tension someone else throws our way, we can still stay open, even when it hurts. In fact taking on tensions means we may sometimes feel as though we are burning up inside. Still we don't talk about it; we just do it. We also don't come back later and say, "Remember what I did for you?"

All you really have to do for others is love them and extend to them the respect that allows them to have their own complications. That is enough. When I meet people who are complicated and unhappy I don't shed tears for them. Rather I am simply happy to see them. It is my experience that if you feel sorry for others, then they feel sorry for themselves too, and withdraw. Despite your intentions to help, you inadvertantly feed a sense of separation. On the other hand if you give people love, they respond. People need love, not pity. Then they can grow and change.

The point is to love someone else and to be joyous for him or her, no matter what. Actually, *true* love is to be happy ourselves, no matter what, because to hold onto complex feelings for others is only a way of limiting ourselves. Then what kind of help can we really be?

Genuine love is about taking on tension and translating it into a creative flow. Instead of giving advice, love is often a matter of buttoning our lip and doing something real for someone else. *What* to do will become apparent from the circumstances.

The effect of this is an environment in which others can begin to recover their own balance by clearly seeing someone who doesn't react to a lot of tension. If *we* react, it only makes the whole situation crazier. So we don't react, even if another person is being totally unreasonable.

This doesn't mean that we turn into wimps, or that we give in to something to which we don't subscribe; it *does* mean that we don't get all tense in response to it. If we can become quiet and centered in those moments, even when somebody is driving staves through us and generating the most painful of circumstances, then our calmness and centeredness will help the other person to change his or her approach.

This may not happen right away. A person will either become more intense, or settle down. But those who become more intense will exhaust themselves pretty soon. Once someone settles down, then there may be a chance for a real rapport to develop.

What we are *not* doing is feeding the fire or causing the other person to become more agitated and tense. By settling things down in ourselves, we allow someone else to begin to see the real choices that are available. This allows the other person to think about what he or she wants to be like. All of this is a powerful and important message to give to somebody else. It is a message that few people ever really have the chance to receive, but one that is vital and life-giving. This is what makes it love.

# Loving Life Itself

LIVING a life from love may not always answer the question "What's going to happen to me?" Indeed it may raise the question more often than it ever answers it. But I have never really concerned myself with that, because in the long run I have always found that making decisions or actions from love always ends up benefiting me extraordinarily. In the short term it may change my life in ways I have no capacity to anticipate; it may even cause me to suffer some discomfort.

At the same time, it saves me from a lot of pain and suffering in the long term. It certainly saves me from a lot of self-rejection. So I would say that although keeping your heart open every single day and trying to love the people around you may seem like an elementary place to start, it can change you in ways that are hard to imagine.

To strive to be loving people — if we do so with awareness — informs every aspect of our behavior. The way to think about this endeavor is to ask ourselves whether we are taking care of ourselves in a narrow sense, or taking care of an event as a whole. In our heart of hearts, what are we *really* thinking about and serving? When we ask ourselves the question honestly, we may find that we are swimming around in these personal interests a lot more than we thought.

With what do we identify? We can come back to the discussion of what it is that we love. Do we love our own personal interests or do we love something deeper? Are we only taking care of our own interests or are we serving Life Itself? The question is that simple, and everything flows from our answer.

Here is another way of thinking about it: In everybody's life there is accumulation and distribution. This is the nature of Life. But as accumulation and distribution happen, are we attached to the accumulation while resisting the distribution? Are we valuing the getting more than the giving? Do we think we are giving when, in fact, we're really giving with the expectation of getting? All of this is called serving our own interests. On the other hand, to recognize the infinite process of accumulation and distribution and to participate in that process as a whole is to serve Life Itself, because in so doing, everyone is served at once.

We can choose to love the effects of Life Itself and make them our priorities — the people, places, and things in our lives — or we can love their source, and let *that* love inform our whole response to all the particulars. It is like loving another person: We can love what that other person does for us, or what we want him or her to do for us, or what we imagine will be done for us — or we can simply love the person. If we choose to love the effects, then what we are calling love becomes unpredictable and can change. First we love this person, then that one. Loving the effects, we go around looking for the perfect place to put our love (as though there were one). However if we choose to love the person, then we just love. To love Life Itself is something like that.

Wherever we start out in the endeavor to be loving people is all right. We can start out for any reason we want. Then we will observe that some things work, while others don't. We may come to a point where we say, "Being a loving person is stupid." Then we make decisions that cause us to close down. Either that, or we see that being loving people has nothing to do with making money, getting positive feedback, or even feeling better in the short term. We understand that it has everything to do with achieving our maximum potential as human beings. *Then* the reason we choose to be loving people is because we love Life Itself.

This happens through opening ourselves and taking our attention into our hearts. In this way, we release the tensions we find there, thereby allowing a creative flow to assert itself and unwind, level by level. As it does so, it unfolds to articulate a truly extraordinary, pure creative power.

At the heart of this is surrender. At the heart of surrender is the ability to let go of everything we think we are, everything we want, and all that we think we need to do in order to walk through all the fears that keep us locked in a contracted kind of existence. It is by letting go of our tensions and by going beyond our fears that we live in the completeness of the flow of creative energy within ourselves that is the perfection of Life.

This process requires the capacity for a simple, sustained effort. This is our real challenge. I love to talk about sweetness and light, but the fact of the matter is that, in order to attain the sweetness implicit in the ripening and maturity of our own lives, we have to face a lot of tensions, fears, and fundamental doubts about ourselves that are inherent in our existence as individuals.

Only in transforming our tensions and facing the fears — only in observing and understanding the mechanism within us through which the simple, pure presence of Life Itself manifests in our lives — do we finally arrive at the shores of creation and attain an enduring sweetness and peace. The sweetness is what dissolves the distinction between the good years and the bad; it is what enables us to live with both.

To do this takes the capacity to approach our lives with love for, and devotion to, Life Itself. We train ourselves to stay open, no matter what dance the world around us is doing. Whether that dance looks terrifying or alluring, it is up to us to stay within the awareness of our own creative flow, allowing that flow to extend itself day by day, no matter what. If we deeply invest our energy in our own growth, then instead of having some good years and some bad ones, we will have only extraordinary times.

Regardless of what happens in the world around us, the possibility for an ever-deepening discovery of our Self is always present and compelling. The possibilities of going beyond every misunderstanding of who and what

we are is enormous. The point is to be serious and committed about growing as human beings. In doing so, we
discover how to shape every level of our lives into a
wonderful extension of the possibilities for discovering
and living in the truth.

Surrender is the key. Through our inner work, along
with continuous devotion and dedication, slowly we
experience and understand what it means to live in that
awareness all the time. The attainment of this understanding is what makes our lives rich and sweet, and
every day filled with miracle.

# Pain, Anger, and Compassion

*Discovering our integrity has nothing
to do with anger against any other.
Real integrity involves recognizing who
and what we are. We then live in that
awareness in the context of tolerance for
everybody else.*

# Pain and Love

TRANSFORMING tensions is not possible without some degree of pain. Everything has a price, and every loving experience we have ever had and ever hope to have will include pain. To think that we can love without pain is profoundly immature. If we understand this as we enter any relationship, then when pain comes, it is not a reason to end the relationship. Pain in no way diminishes the love; it is part of the transformative experience that comes from loving.

There are two aspects to pain. The first is the pain we feel when we learn the limits of others; the second is the pain we feel when we recognize our own. We must transcend our reaction to both if we are ever to discover the fundamental oneness of Life. This is so, because pain and love are two sides of the pure experience of Life Itself, and both will come to us if we are truly growing.

We can think of it like this: Love is an endless pouring forth. In its universal sense it is an infinite giving of itself. We can think of pain as the opposite of this pouring forth. It is a kind of contraction, a pulling back. The two are intrinsically related. So we cannot experience love unless we can also experience pain. They are two aspects of what we call Life, and they always go together.

Furthermore, this is not a pessimistic view. As the tide pours onto the beach it changes the structure of the beach; as it pulls back, it reveals its change. As it pours forth and pulls back over and over again, it is simply expressing itself, demonstrating its vitality, genius, and brilliance.

Life always expresses itself as this kind of pulsation between extension and contraction. One is always hidden in the other, just as happiness and sadness are always hidden within one another. No amount of intellectualizing is ever going to separate them or resolve the fundamental tension between the two. It is a universal paradox that is unresolvable at the level of thought.

Yet it is not necessary to resolve this paradox, because it is not a problem. Rather it is part of the vitality from which the whole world flows. Each time you let go, enter deeply into this essential tension between expansion and contraction within yourself, and open yourself to it, you penetrate the paradox and encounter what lies at its core. At the heart of that essential tension you discover the authentic vitality of your own life and of Life Itself.

Growing spiritually is the process of finding and keeping your balance in the midst of that tension. First you find your own balance, even in the middle of the pain; then you find the balance at the heart of *every* paradox. Learning to do this teaches you that pain is nothing more than change. It is the way our systems express their response to their own self-transformation. We feel pain whenever love is trying to bring about a change, and our egos are busy trying to resist it. Some part of us doesn't want to do the inner work required to grow, so we feel pain. However when we can also recognize it as something wonderful, it doesn't totally dominate our nervous systems or make us crazy with suffering. It's just pain.

Let's face it. If we cut a finger, it may be intensely painful but it doesn't drive us into a frenzy. We just clean it and tape it up. Even if we whack off the finger with a chain-saw, we still do basically the same thing. We clean it, we wrap it, and then we get over it. It is the deeper pain of not knowing what is going to happen to us that causes us to translate pain into suffering. *That* is what makes us feel crazy. That is the pain we are not sure we will get over. The point of our inner work is to learn to digest all of it and to grow from the process.

Each of us in our close relationships lives every single day with some pain. For that matter, there is always a certain amount of pain and some sense of distance between ourselves and others — even with the people we love the most. If we are not to be overwhelmed by that pain or become totally reactive to it, if we are not to act out a life that has nothing to do with the real opportunity in front of us but only with a myopic understanding of the pain, then we have to find something within ourselves that will lift us above that pain. This comes, once again, from opening our hearts. It is that simple. When we open our hearts, we find everything we need.

When I am in pain I turn my attention inside by focusing on opening my heart. As I do so, I feel within myself for the simple sweetness and joy that is within my own heart and, more deeply, within my soul. This is what takes me beyond the pain. It doesn't fix any problem. In a way, it solves nothing — and yet it makes everything different. This is true for each of us.

The practice of opening our hearts doesn't change the fact that we are still ourselves. We still have our own life's work to do and our own life's challenges to face. But because we are no longer reacting to the pain of our circumstances, we live our lives permeated with the awareness of our interconnectedness with those around us, and full of appreciation for that interconnectedness. Then we are not building walls around ourselves or becoming increasingly isolated.

This takes practice. We cannot be expected to know automatically how to do it. At the same time, when we work to let go and open our hearts over and over and over again, it simply becomes a way of life. What we are doing is appreciating, giving back to, and fully participating in the process that we call love.

The experience of love is what heals the pain. It doesn't resolve any dilemmas or fix any problems, but it does heal them so that we can see them differently. Then they're fine, finished, and we get on with our lives. When we understand this, then even when we feel pain continuously we can also recognize it as a manifestation of a deeper life within us, for which we can be grateful.

# Peeling Away the Illusions

$P$ARADOXICALLY, pain and love are basically the same thing: strong energy that is in some way attempting to get our attention and communicate some information to us. We only experience it as pain when we are not prepared to handle it. A lot of this pain comes from having to face the mistakes we have made in our relationships with others. Yet some of the most important lessons I have ever learned in my life came from the most painful mistakes I have made.

To feel pain, in a way, is Life telling us, "Here is an opportunity to learn — you can turn into a stump, or you can wake up even more and become a stronger, bigger person." We get to choose. Will we become stumps? Will we simply shut down further, shield ourselves from that information, and respond to the pain by saying, "I will never let myself be hurt again"?

Will we close ourselves down more and more tightly as we go along until we are basically brain-dead, with little operating in there besides hormones? Or, when we bump into painful situations, will we see that the first thing we have to do is try to open ourselves (even to our mistakes), find our center, and recover our balance?

We have to be free to make mistakes and open enough within ourselves to do so. We don't have to hate ourselves for our mistakes, because we are not required to be perfect in this life (or at least not in the first fifteen tries). At the same time, we do have to find a place within ourselves that can open and start to take in the information that comes to us from these mistakes, thereby allowing it to change us.

Suppose, for example, that our feelings get hurt. To open and accept that information doesn't mean we resolve that the so-and-so who did it will never get away with it again. Taking in the information should not cause us to become cynical or hardened. Instead we are taking it in to learn more about ourselves and to become more skillful and thoughtful people.

As we observe these things, gradually we come to experience the pressures operating in our lives not as "my boyfriend, my girlfriend, my lack of a boyfriend or girlfriend, my money, my lack of money, my job, my lack of a job, my career, my lack of a career," but simply as different kinds of energy. Our minds may put labels on them, but even then the labels rarely have anything to do with what we think they do.

Paradoxically most of the pain we feel also has little to do with what we think is hurting us. What really happens is that, as we start to change, different experiences and circumstances begin to break away from the surface of our awareness. As they break away, we start shouting and trying to hold on. But the whole drama we create is about what is happening only on the surface of our experience. It is different from the deeper level on which the real change is taking place.

Even when we think we can identify the cause and effect of our pain, we are usually looking at the wrong cause and effect. We don't see that a new life within us is coming into being — a new awakening trying to take place. In itself, this process hurts. So if we identify with what is actually the superficial drama, then we neglect this deeper dimension and never let it get off the ground. Instead we direct all our attention to circumstances outside ourselves, trying to pinpoint their part in our pain.

In my own relationships with people, I assume that I have no idea who I am really dealing with for a long time. For me, the discovery process takes years, and I think that's true for everybody else as well. It takes time to get to know somebody.

During that time, it is easy for us to let our illusions take over and dominate our ideas about somebody else. As soon as that happens, however, we are not really carrying on a relationship with another person, but only with our own illusions. In fact the other person as a real, living, breathing individual pretty much falls out the bottom. Yet when our illusions fail us, we throw out the person onto whom we've projected them. We gather up our illusions and march off to play someplace else. "You broke my heart, and now I'm going to find someone who will not."

That never gets us anywhere. It was our illusions that were the problem in the first place, and never the other person. For that matter other people are pretty straightforward about what they are, even when they don't mean to be. For the careful observer, everybody is presenting themselves clearly all the time.

So we have to think about what we want and what we are expecting from our relationships. I do believe that relationships are about stability, companionship, and the possibility of some deeply shared experience. But any relationship is meaningful only in direct proportion to the depth of our rapport with ourselves. That equation we will find to be universally true. We determine the nature of our relationships based upon our rapport with ourselves.

There will always be cases when we should have known better. Whenever I get my feelings hurt and see that I've made a mistake, what hurts the most is that the basic information was already there, and that I should have known all along that I was involved in a stupid situation. It's not what the other person did that really hurts; it's realizing that in some way I blinded myself to something I should have seen.

So what usually hurts the most is recognizing that we could have avoided a situation entirely if we hadn't been so involved in our own illusions. As we let ourselves see these things, and as a lot of these illusions peel away, we become much clearer about who we are and what Life is. To a big degree this allows for tremendous refinement and flexibility in the way we express our lives.

This translates into a way of life that has little to do with what is ordinary or normal, because true flexibility and strength of creative expression have little to do with what many people bring to life. Most of us want certainty and definition — that is, control. We want to *know* how we really feel and then try to keep everything just the same. This is not possible.

It is better to take in the energy of each situation, even when it is painful to do so, and let it show us something about ourselves. This can only make each of us a bigger person. We understand that it is a wonderful thing to have our illusions peeled away for the two or three hundredth time, until we finally get over them. We start to see ourselves and others as we all really are. Then we can let everybody, including ourselves, just *be*. Moreover what we end up with is something wonderful.

At the same time, what we end up with is not exactly something personal. When I say this, most people get a little nervous. We cannot easily imagine an experience that isn't "personal," so we tend to be a little scared by the idea. But how do we know if it frightens us until we've actually done it? It is sort of like standing at the top of a mountain. Until we've done it, we have no idea just how far-reaching the space around us can be. That experience alone enlarges our vision of everything enormously.

In this case, it means that we look to understand love by going beyond an idea of "self" based on our narrow identification with our individuality. Doing so enlarges our vision of things, and makes us see everything differently. So until we've jumped out of the personal into a bigger vision, how do we really know if it frightens us or not? Going beyond the personal does not mean that we cease to operate as individuals; it does not mean that we stop having relationships with other people; it is not about becoming cold or impersonal. Quite the opposite. It means that we explore a love without limits, and do everything we can to articulate that love through the medium of our individual lives. Letting go of our illusions is one of the ways we become able to do this.

# Pain and Anger

$O$FTEN we respond to pain with anger. In recent years
this has become more culturally acceptable, as people
have been encouraged to review all the things that happened to them as they were growing up and to become
aware of all the things about which they are still angry.
We are encouraged to know when we are angry and,
more to the point, to express that anger to whomever we
feel is responsible for provoking it.

I have always found, however, that whatever tension
I unload on another person is a tension I myself will have
to eat in the long run — without fail. This is because what
we put out usually goes forth more simply than what
eventually comes back around to smack us in the face.
Each person who passes it on usually throws in a few
additional tensions of his or her own, thereby compound-
ing the original problem. This is why I am committed to

digesting something the first time around instead of passing it on for fifteen people to add to it before it gets back to me — because it always comes back.

Like any tension, anger is just strong energy that erupts out of our concern for what *has* happened to us or what *may* happen to us in a situation. If we take that energy and dump it either on somebody else or back on ourselves, we only strengthen and reinforce the fundamental situation that frustrated us in the first place. We may feel we have to let go of it by releasing it in somebody else's direction, but in my view that is not the best thing to do.

Instead we want to do the counter-intuitive thing and learn to take our attention deeper within ourselves, to open ourselves in new ways. This is not at all easy, and sometimes we are going to feel as though we are burning up in the process. What is really happening, however, is that we are penetrating old patterns that have become established within and around us.

As we do so, once again we discover the profound and dynamic stillness at our very core. In the process, we give our old patterns a new center — that core of stillness — around which to organize themselves. Doing so allows a real change in our overall perception to occur. This gives us a flexibility and range of creative expression that is much vaster than before, so that we find ourselves to be less limited.

Whether we recognize it or not, we are part of a bigger unified system. Our whole life is a system, and each of our connections to everyone and everything else is part of that system. We are not the separate beings we often imagine ourselves to be. If we spit out some energy as tension, it is going to bounce from one part of the system to another until it finally bounces back to us. This is the nature of a system. It is only when we start to digest that tension ourselves that we become free to participate in the system on a whole different level.

There is not a day when life will start being better on its own. It gets better because *we* decide we want to grow as human beings and because we start to understand the real source of this growth. We recognize that growing is not about the accumulation of things or about the addition of relationships to our lives. Rather we grow from our contact with our own heart of hearts, and from opening and expanding that heart every single day. Our lives get better from the richness we feel within ourselves and the generosity with which we express that richness, irrespective of what other people say and do.

There are really only two people in this world with whom we can get angry: the other person, or ourselves. What good does either one do? When we can go beyond the immediate events, we see that whatever happened, in a deeper sense, is nobody's fault. This is a hard thing to accept, because we always *want* everything to be somebody else's fault. Still this is not possible. Why? Because people are usually either speaking out of their own pain or acting out of their fear that the available resources are too limited and they aren't going to get enough. Think of the occasions when you have done things that angered other people. Was this not the case?

Thus the issue is not one of getting angry. Whenever you find yourself getting mad at all, it should ring a bell for you so that you can say, "Hey, what am I doing?" Then you stop, take a breath, and start to work more deeply within yourself to let go of the tension. Anything else only directs your energy back into some form of self-justification, and acts to make the ego more rigid and defensive.

To work more deeply within yourself, sit down, pull back your shoulders to loosen them, relax and wiggle your jaw a little bit, and start working in yourself to open your heart. Notice your breathing, and let all the compression within you release, thereby returning it to its real state as energy. Then it can start to flow freely again through your whole mechanism.

As you release the tension, you allow it to become creative energy once again. As you open yourself to absorb that energy, it will become a whole different level of resource so that you don't have to just spit it out as anger. In the process, it will reorganize your entire system.

We can either allow our anger to get stuck — in which case it only becomes another wrapping in the cocoon of our individuality — or we can open ourselves to it deeply, become aware of it as energy, recover the creative aspect of that energy, and become stronger from it. In short, once again, we can open our hearts.

It always seems so much more satisfying to blow off steam. The question in the long run, however, is what kind of people we want to become. Do we want the short-term gratification of blowing off steam, or do we want to become people capable of understanding and managing our energy in a deeply thoughtful way? In doing the latter we learn how to be skillful givers — and there is no doubt that our lives among people require us to be skillful.

What we discover in the process is that fear and anger are two sides of the same coin. Fear is what happens when we take strong energy out on ourselves; anger is when we take it out on somebody else. If we can cultivate new ways of addressing both our fear and our anger, we become extraordinarily steady, strong people. Then we are able to develop a broader and broader perspective on whatever system we are operating in. Ultimately to do so frees us from being confined by the limits of that system. This is what love and growing are really about.

Sometimes our lives appear to give us endless cause for bitterness and anger. We could build whole cities out of it. Yet only when we learn to let go — only when we let the deeper life within us unfold in its own way — will our anger ever really resolve and the love we have sought all along become apparent to us.

# Transforming Anger

THERE are times when we may have something important to say to someone else. In that case we first digest our own emotions and chemistry, taking the powerful energy we feel, circulating it through ourselves, and absorbing it deeply. After that we can sit down together and say in a simple way, "Look, this and this happened, and it really bothered me. I would like to talk about it." Then we can listen to what the other person has to say without getting into an argument.

We have to make sure we're ready to talk about something without spewing or venting. If we can't do that, then it is better just to wait and continue to work in the situation until we can speak clearly.

Don't get me wrong — if the situation calls for it, I may raise my voice and get noisy. I have no problem with getting loud sometimes if somebody is not listening. But I don't mix that with anger, because that combination goes nowhere useful.

The minute we allow the anger to take over, we are not in charge any more. Anger is in charge, and anger says what is going to happen. Then the laws and chemistry of anger prevail, and not our reason, intelligence, compassion, or any deeper part of us. Once we make that choice, the rules of the anger game take over.

When we have feelings of anger, what is important is not that we try to change the feelings themselves, but that we change our level of identification with them. If the feelings come up and we identify with them, then we usually end up working ourselves into a bigger and bigger head of steam. The next thing we know, we're dumping it on the next poor person who walks by. Then that person — who was probably just going along minding his or her own business in the first place — gets splattered.

The alternative is to say to ourselves, "Hmm, there is some anger present here," and to let ourselves relax about it. We make the effort to keep our attention inside, stay open, and find our center. Then the anger can reorganize itself, and we have the possibility of doing something progressive with it.

I am not talking about suppressing anything, but about *transforming* it. In one sense, the very act of maintaining an awareness of our emotions acts as a subtle suppression. But it is not a matter of cranking down our emotions and closing them off. Rather it is a subtle stepping back that introduces a little bit of a delay. Just doing that causes our own creative energy to transform itself, and to become more powerful and clear.

We can notice that we are angry. We can also remain aware that, ultimately, we don't really want to be angry. This, in turn, comes from a resolve to grow and to maintain a certain environment within ourselves. With that resolve in mind, when we observe something coming up that is not really conducive to an inner environment of openness, we can take the steps necessary to re-establishing our inner balance.

Much of the time people seek to maintain their sense of balance in external ways by creating one identity or another. "I am a member of this or that, I am this or that kind of person." Then they spend a lot of energy defending these boundaries and getting angry when other people don't recognize them. But when we can let these identities become less important, and focus instead on sustaining our inner balance, then real transformation takes place. This has nothing to do with repressing or suppressing anything.

When we feel strong energies building up within us, it may take us a while to absorb and release them within ourselves. We may not be able to digest them immediately. So we give them time. When I talk about not venting anger, I am not suggesting any particular prohibition against anger itself. What I am talking about is what we *do* with it. In any situation that confronts us, it is better to think carefully about what the whole situation is really about. We want to respond to the situation itself, instead of getting entangled in all the specific interactions and losing sight of what we are trying to do in the bigger picture.

This requires a certain vigilance. When we catch ourselves handling things in less than admirable ways, the only thing we can do is start being vigilant again.

After all, what are our choices? We can either shoot ourselves, go back to sleep, or start over again. I'd say that starting over again is probably the best thing.

Sometimes we may have to start over again many times. That is not the issue. Remaining vigilant is the issue, and this is a capacity we cultivate through repeated practice. Jeláluddin Rumi, the thirteenth century Turkish poet and mystic, had a sign over the entry to his spiritual community that said something like this: "Come, come to the semma, come again. Even if you've broken your vows a thousand times, come again. Ours is not a caravan of despair."

# Forgiveness and Tolerance

*T*HE perspective I am taking on anger is not a popular one. Still it has been my observation and experience that anger is the expression not of spirit, but of ego. On the personal level, it reduces us to the level of whatever we are struggling with; at the level of inner stillness, it becomes irrelevant.

The example of Jesus's anger in the temple is sometimes used to illustrate anger expressed in the service of love. Interestingly this view is not necessarily shared by other spiritual traditions. For example, in early commentaries by the Japanese on their perception of the Christians, Jesus's anger was seen as disqualifying the claims of his divinity. From the Buddhist and Shinto perspectives, a spiritual person does not show anger but, instead, compassion and openness toward others. For that matter, the appropriate expression of Christianity is tolerance, charity, and forgiveness. "Forgive them — they know not what they do."

Forgiveness and compassion may seem to lie beyond anything we can manage. It may be that we have grown up in circumstances that have left us completely out of touch with our feelings. So we may feel that becoming aware of how we *really* feel — especially uncovering our anger — is tremendously important. To some degree this may be true.

However if we are truly committed to growing as spiritual people and to developing inner mastery, then we cannot linger in this stage for very long. It is too costly in terms of our own integrity and equilibrium. It puts us at risk of becoming precisely what we are against. Moreover discovering our integrity has nothing to do with anger against any *other*. Real integrity involves recognizing who and what *we* are. We then live out that awareness in the context of tolerance for everybody else.

From the point of view of some of the different Eastern spiritual traditions, a person of great virtue is one who lives with immense patience and tolerance of others. This makes anger a poor substitute for real self-awareness. In venting it, we reduce ourselves to the level of that which repels us, entering into a greater pattern of imbalance.

People who approach others in anger often unconsciously want to make victims out of those who have victimized them — to change positions with what was oppressing them in the first place — even when they think they are only trying to bring about equality. So they may feel some initial rush of gratification in this expression of personal power. This is an important transition point. That sense of personal power can easily expand into a whole life pattern, in which the person who was victimized comes to occupy the very position of dominance he or she was once trying to escape.

The approach I am proposing is a long-term one. A person who is really concerned with growing spiritually must think in terms of the big picture and the long-term effects of his or her actions. It is my feeling that our starting point always informs where we end up. To start with anger cannot help but lead to further anger. Struggle begets struggle.

When we learn to operate on a different level, however — a level that is possible when we learn what it means to open our hearts and feel the deeper connection between ourselves and others — then we see how short-term the benefits of venting anger truly are. In the context of a greater openness, it turns out to be not the expression of openness so many people think it is, but the closing off of possibilities we cannot imagine unless we operate from the logic of love.

The logic of love teaches us to remain open, no matter what — especially when we would prefer to stay closed. Was this, perhaps, what Jesus had in mind when he taught his followers to turn the other cheek?

# Compassion

$I$T IS not always easy to see things from somebody else's point of view. When it is not, we may just have to accept that the other person is acting out of his or her own tensions and need, and that we can't be too involved one way or the other. We don't have to close our hearts, get angry, or make accusations. Compassion, in such a case, is simply a matter of acceptance in the biggest sense.

Our lives in the world engage all of us in a basic struggle for survival in which we act out our biological imperatives to eat and reproduce. Most of us are conditioned by all our experiences to identify with these biological imperatives and all the tensions they generate, without understanding the infinite nature of our inner resources. This being so, it becomes a little easier to see what the difficulties in living are about, and to have a basic compassion from which we can operate. Beginning with a broad understanding of the struggle of humanity, we can bring it down to the specific situation.

This in no way relieves us from the need to do our own inner work; nor does it eliminate the possibility that frictions will emerge within our environment. It doesn't make it any less necessary to hold to our personal convictions, even as we try to find a balance point from which to create a consensus in whatever relationship we find ourselves.

Compassion does not make us mushy-headed; it doesn't require us to abandon our principles or to become weak. Only a strong person can genuinely discover that balance from which every human being's highest best interest extends.

Compassion is an aspect of understanding. When we really know the nature of our own hearts, then we are naturally compassionate toward other people. That compassion comes from the recognition that we have done many stupid things in our own lives that have made us suffer and caused others to suffer as well.

If we have been able to get past our own stupidity, then when we are exposed to the suffering and stupidity of others, we are better able to be patient with them. Our interactions are then more likely to facilitate others' going beyond their own stuckness. Because we see ourselves in others, we strive to support them in this process. We understand that by doing so we are also freeing ourselves.

This compassion can take many forms. Sometimes it is a helping hand; sometimes it is a strong response. Either way, it is not useful to *try* to be compassionate. It is better just to be ourselves. If we can do that, then our natural compassion will come through. It must.

We demonstrate our awareness of compassion every single day by transforming our own tensions and allowing our creative energy to flow freely. To do this is the real way we give to the situation in which we find ourselves. We are thereby learning and growing, and expressing love and surrender.

This kind of growth is something that happens within us and that we demonstrate all around us. In the field of our lives we demonstrate it as service — to ourselves, our families, our communities, our society and nation, to our planet — indeed, to Life Itself in all its expressions. Ultimately we are talking about our *participation* in Life Itself.

Along with compassion must come respect. Genuine respect for everybody is essential. This is not a moral stance. It is simply the recognition that whatever we encounter in somebody else is an expression of the same Life that expresses itself through us. When we understand that every human being is an amazing creative power, full of surprises, then we don't have any wrong assumptions about our relationships to one another. In that case, real love and respect can grow. This is the only need we really have, if we can even call it a need. All our other ideas about what we need are essentially empty, because even when we attain the specific thing we had in mind, we still haven't gotten what we really wanted in the first place.

Out of love and respect for ourselves and others, we don't put our tensions on anybody else. Instead we learn about surrender. We think a lot about it and try to understand it, because out of our understanding of surrender a state of openness emerges. Our hearts and minds become open and, in that openness, we begin to perceive the thread that unites one person and another in the divine dance of creation.

As we begin to sense that thread and develop a real feeling for it, slowly we begin to understand it. Gradually we grasp its qualities and learn to live in harmony with it, attuned to it. As we follow it, it expands our perspective, our understanding, our deepest intuition, and our inner sense to the point of finally encompassing the unity of Life Itself. In that unity, we are not necessarily free from pain, but we *are* free from suffering.

Life is not about what we want. Life is about how we take what we've got and find a way to make it wonderful. So in all the changes we go through in our lives, it is important to cling to the love and respect we have for ourselves and that we profess as our value for Life Itself. When we live from love and respect, we will go through every change and only be uplifted by it. As we grow and change, we will find that we grow closer to the things that are really important to us.

A person who experiences the fullness of his or her own creative energy can only demonstrate tolerance, patience, openness, persistence, love, and respect toward his or her fellow human beings. This is no cliché, nor is it anything we can fake, because real love and respect, as well as true patience and tolerance, always test us. They give us the opportunity to demonstrate the degree to which we really understand the fullness within us.

So in our interactions with those whose lives touch ours, love and respect are what define the parameters of our creative expression. They operate as guidelines for what we will and will not do, giving us the opportunity to find harmony and balance, and to discover an appropriateness of action in all the areas in which we want to express ourselves.

First we learn to know our own hearts. In so doing, we discover the deeper life that connects us all, which is the real source of all love and respect. As we deepen our understanding of this source, we extend our awareness of it into all the different realms of our experience. More and more, we meet it in everyone and everything we encounter. It then becomes a foundation, a reference point, and an understanding on which we hang our hats. Then we cannot get lost, regardless of what Life Itself calls us to do.

# Boundaries and Exchange

*Our love for another opens us to an experience of exchange. That exchange allows us to experience the creative power within us, and the renewal implicit in that creative power.*

# Dissolving Boundaries

THERE is definitely a level on which boundaries are always appropriate. We can't have creative expression in an environment of confusion. Our lives take on a scope, a scale, and a dynamic in proportion to the appropriate channels of communication we are able to establish with others. If we cannot establish the boundaries necessary to make that communication possible, we cannot sustain our contact with a deeper sense of quality and depth in our own lives. Thus many of the boundaries that people talk about needing to establish to correct dysfunctions in their relationships and their environments are, on this level, a necessary thing.

We have to have the ability to live disciplined lives. This requires that we know our limits. Then we are not chasing wildly after one thing or another, but investing our energy thoughtfully and thereby developing ourselves. This is important, because as we come together as human beings, many opportunities present themselves for us to go in many directions. As we become whole, all kinds of other people want to talk to us. So it is necessary to have a sense of what we can handle and what we cannot.

On another level, however, the life of a spiritual person is about dissolving boundaries. What do I mean? Some of the boundaries we try to set are really expressions of our resistance to change and to growing. Most of this resistance actually has nothing to do with anybody else's problems. Instead, it has to do with our own need to grow.

When we live lives oriented by the wish to grow, then the appropriate boundaries in our lives — whether these be emotional, psychological, or physical — are defined not in the negative intention of keeping one thing or another *out*, but by directing the flow of our creative energy toward our larger aim. Because we are committed to being the best people we can possibly be, we no longer have time to pursue a lot of dead ends. So the boundaries in our lives become defined in a positive way: "I will not beat up on that person, because I am too busy trying to become established in an attitude of love and respect to beat up on anybody."

Everyone lives within parameters. The discussion of dissolving our boundaries has nothing to do with a lack of parameters. Rather we discover that there is nothing we won't do to promote our authentic growth, strength, and clarity. This does *not* mean that we no longer say no to anything we are asked to do. It does mean that when growing is our objective, we have a different way of assessing what we can and cannot do. By looking at a situation and asking ourselves about the highest best interest of all involved, we become more capable of a subtle discrimination. We can see what will further our inner work and our ability to serve, and what will not. Understanding these things, we become willing to work in whatever way we are called to work and to serve however we are asked to serve.

These things are important. If we don't learn to release the boundaries that keep us from loving what we are, we will never find out what it is we have to give in this life. Since our ability to love and our ability to give freely without counting the cost are one and the same thing, testing and dissolving the boundaries that constrain us are necessary to living out the logic of love.

# The Oneness of Love

WHEN I was twenty-three years old my spiritual teacher, Rudi, passed away. Once a month, for the six months before, he had told me that it would happen, and I hadn't believed him. Then it happened anyway. I loved him more than I had ever loved anyone else before and more than I have loved anyone since, and suddenly he was gone.

I was asked by his family to go to the funeral home to view the body and to approve all the arrangements for the funeral. So I went and discovered, to my surprise, that there wasn't a single moment of pain for me in the whole experience. Even today, almost twenty years later, I have no pain from it. I looked at the body and saw not one glimmer of anything related to Rudi. It was just a body and there was no issue.

Love and loving are not about bodies, or even about our lives as individuals. I had been with Rudi for almost two years. His death was the perfect opportunity for me to feel that life had proved itself to be terrible after all. Instead of thinking that, however, I continued to love him and to discover love.

This experience is what led me to understand that loving and life are not connected to bodies. Bodies are only an effect of Life. What is most deeply alive never dies, and neither does real love. What I loved about Rudi was not even Rudi himself, exactly, but what happened to me in his company because of the quality of love that he *was*. That was the truly amazing experience, and I loved that. To one degree or another, this is what happens to us in the company of anyone we love. We cultivate that experience, look at it carefully, take care of it, and let it grow inside us. This is what makes it possible for us to become big enough people to love in a real way.

What do I mean by this? Real love is not about who or what we are as individual expressions of Life. The experience of love transcends all the information of our senses. It has nothing to do with what we see, hear, say, smell, or touch. It is not a question of rejecting, denying, or suppressing this information, but of going beyond it to recognize the oneness of the love that underlies the whole universe. Then we discover that all the boundaries we assume between ourselves and others do not, in fact, really exist. There *is* no real boundary, but only one thing. That is why I say that real love is not personal. I mean that it is in no way limited.

I spent years looking for the boundary between me and Rudi; I couldn't find it. Indeed, when Rudi passed away, all I could do at first was look for him. I was looking for *his* boundary in order to get past my own. After a while, it dawned on me that Rudi was right there with me and that I didn't need to look anyplace else. Then I started looking for the boundaries to *that* experience, until I discovered again that there were none there, either. That is how big love really is.

# Exchange

W H E N E V E R we have a conversation with another person, a flow takes place. On the simplest level, this involves a flow of information. The more we attune ourselves to the interchange, however, the more we realize that an interchange is happening on other levels as well. The more obvious of these are things like body language, the emotional overtones, and the levels of tension or ease we communicate to one another.

The less obvious aspect involves an exchange on the level of energy. This is analogous to placing two magnets near each other. Their exchange of electrons is perceived as the exchange of energy. In our own contact with others, we exchange energy with everyone in ways that promote or disturb the balance we are always seeking.

Energy exchanges are constantly taking place. I sometimes use the analogy of a weather system to suggest that atmospheric equilibrium is brought about as the atmosphere attempts to find a balance within itself. Because heat, light, and moisture differ at all the different points on the globe, many dynamics are going on simultaneously, all of them trying to move toward an equilibrium.

In a basic way, everything we do in our everyday world is nothing but the exchange of energy. Even the purpose of our biological imperatives — eating and reproducing — is the exchange of energy. Everything in which we engage is part of this exchange, from our most abstract conversations to going to the bathroom in the morning. From the simplest to the most sophisticated level of manifestation, we are continuously exchanging with our environment.

As we examine more and more carefully the fundamental process of exchange which is the basis of even the crudest aspects of our material existence, we realize that the whole thing is nothing but energy. At first we may think it's money, food, and other things we pass back and forth. When we look more closely at the whole picture, however, we see that all these things are simply expressions of energy. The exchange of energy is what Life is really about. Moreover, it is not as though there are a lot of separate energies interacting. At the deepest level, it is all the energy of Life Itself, expressing itself in many ways, each of them interacting with each other. Although it looks like many things, at the deepest level, there is only this one reality.

As we become increasingly aware of our own participation in this exchange, we become more and more aware of ourselves as a system of energy within a larger network of energy. We start to be able to *feel* this energy of Life in all things, and to recognize it as the same thing, regardless of its forms. Gradually the assumptions we have about our individual identities and their boundaries melt away. Our ideas about others change, too. We begin to recognize how we have held on to illusions and delusions about our separateness, even as these misunderstandings fall away. This recognition, in turn, permits a deeper and deeper level of exchange to take place.

We encounter the infiniteness of our own inner resource, of our own inner Self. We see that the medium in which the whole world is played out is one, not many, and that we are an integral part of the whole. We discover the pointlessness of trying to control others and recognize, instead, the fundamental freedom of all things.

These are not things we have to *think* our way through, because as we open ourselves to our lives, they unfold into an awareness that we simply come to have. This awareness emerges within us as we dissolve our various tensions and insecurities. It unfolds as we become established in the depth of our own being, in the openness of our own hearts.

# Communion

So WHAT does love mean for us? It has multiple levels of meaning, but basically they all refer to one thing, and that is, again, the experience of exchange. Whether we are talking about amorous, sexual, romantic love, or universal love, all are related to the process of exchange. Even when we talk about loving God, we are really talking about participating in the process of exchange at the finest and highest level that we are — the level of communion.

Any true process of communion is one of surrendering our boundaries and limitations, and coming together in exchange, expansion, and unfolding. Our love for another opens us to an experience of exchange. That exchange is a flow which dissolves our tensions and removes the poisons and frustrations from our systems.

It allows us to experience the creative power within us, and the renewal implicit in that creative power.

What we are really looking for underneath all our pursuits is a way to release the tensions, limitations, restrictions, and boundaries within us. We want something that will allow us to participate in that fully unfolded, highest aspect of our own being. Then what we talk about as love is nothing but the experience of the infinity of our own awareness. That is love.

That infinity encompasses everybody and everything. In a practical, pragmatic, worldly level, it requires us to see God in what we think is good and also in what we think is not good. More to the point, it compels us to refrain from judgment — from thinking of someone as a good person and someone else as a bad one.

Free of this kind of confusion, we can see people as they really are, which is a mix. This enables us to let go of many of our concepts and categories, and to encompass those aspects of our own existence that we have been conditioned to believe are inadequate or even bad. We work to integrate all those aspects into our own nature, trying to live in harmony with ourselves as we are, and to recognize that there is no particular requirement for us to behave in any particular way.

As this attitude of self-acceptance grows within us, we become free to release the creative power within us, and to allow it to unfold into the world. This is what frees us to participate in the abundance that *we* are, and to enter into a process of exchange more fully and deeply. It does not give us any license; it does give us liberty. The fact of the matter is that we are free in the beginning, free in the middle, and free in the end.

Freedom is our only condition, really. We are ultimately not limited by social structures, emotional bonds, or any kind of psychological inadequacy. We are not constrained by our past in the slightest. Indeed none of these things defines us. Only to the extent that we identify with them and accept them as limitations do we give them the power to function as something real in our experience.

Surrendering this sense of limitation, restriction, and confining boundaries — even when it feels as though we are going against the grain — we are able to express ourselves in genuine caring that grows out of a much bigger understanding of who and what we are. We are able to exchange and participate in the flow of life with other people, expressing the appropriate respect for them without inappropriate expectations or desires. We are no longer in the relationship business, constantly trying to get something from somebody else. Instead we are free to discover within ourselves the abundance that is there, and to articulate that abundance in the form of a love that is real.

This makes a big difference. All of us know others who ask or demand something of us as though they were entitled to it — and for that reason we will never give it to them in a thousand years. The paradox is that when they don't ask, then there we are, ready to pour it out for free, giving more than they could ever have asked for in the first place.

It is only by recognizing the essential, free state of all human beings that we are able to participate deeply in what is really big and fine within us. This is how we come to recognize and participate in what is big and fine in other people as well. This is the heart of exchange. We don't ignore the peculiarities of others, but we connect to Life on a level deeper than these peculiarities and begin to see how even they are part of an integrated whole. It is a fascinating, fabulous endeavor to recognize that all these peculiarities — and even all the difficulty and unpleasantness in our lives — are fine in and of themselves.

There is something subtle and rich within us that we start to experience. Having encountered this, we find that we stop straining to get hold of people and things outside ourselves. We require no particular recognition, nor is there any particular companionship we crave. In fact, what craving there is no longer leads us around by the nose. It's just there, but our relationship to it becomes entirely different.

In this situation, we come to true realization, renunciation, and fulfillment. All the objectives of orthodox religious endeavors are fulfilled and, at the same time, transcended. We find that there is nothing in this world that we require. Instead our sufficiency is within the divinity of our own awareness. This allows us to love others in the fullness of their freedom, because there is nothing we require them to be for us.

To the extent that we live in this world, our function is to articulate the creative power within us and the freedom that comes from our awareness of it. We are simply *that*. With this understanding we are able to face the uncertainty of our lives and accept what Life offers us. We are able to turn within ourselves and to unfold from our own awareness the highest creative capacity inherent within it. We recognize the treasure within us and are filled by it. Our sufficiency is in that grace — in the absolute fullness of our hearts. Thus in uncertainty we find freedom, and in our freedom, love. This is the nature of communion, the essence of surrender, and the outcome of the logic of love.

# Trust

THERE is a creative power within us that is the foundation of our very existence. From within us, this creative energy spins a whole web that makes up the fabric of our lives. No outer power does that; it is an inner higher power with a dynamic of its own that goes beyond anything we think or anything we want. Usually we sit in judgment of that dynamic as we see it operating in our lives. We say to ourselves, "Oh, this was a good thing, that was a bad thing. Today I'm a good person, but yesterday I wasn't." Yet the whole time we are chattering away to ourselves, the spinning continues. The web extends and contracts, and then extends itself again to manifest its own texture, irrespective of what is going on in our minds.

Surrender is the opening of our hearts that allows us to participate more completely in the dynamic awareness that is both the web and its source. It is what happens when we release tensions and allow our creative energy to flow at the most essential level. It is the discovery that there is something at work beyond our judgments, and that we can trust this something.

As we become more and more deeply relaxed and open within ourselves, the more the source of that spinning becomes apparent to us. We realize that the power of that creative energy and *its* intention are what count, and nothing else. So we learn to release ourselves into that higher power, trust it, and accept from it whatever our life *is*, free of any idea of this being a good thing or that a bad one. None of that matters.

When we are really that free, we can accept from Life whatever it wants to give us, and accept ourselves as we are. Whatever Life brings us we are able to savor, respect, and find joy in it. That's when our lives really start to unfold.

This isn't always easy, and a lot of the time it hurts. There was a sixteenth-century Spanish mystic, St. Teresa of Avila, who once wrote about a dialogue she had with God. She had been having a hard time, and so she said, "God, why am I having so many difficulties?" God said to her, "Oh, because I give difficulties to all my friends." She said, "No wonder you don't have many!"

The question of trust is an essential one. It is not easily resolved in our lives but, as we learn to deal with tensions, it is trust that allows us not to get caught in an event — not to latch onto it or identify with it. Trust is what allows us to turn back and look into ourselves once again, to contemplate and consider our own understanding in the context of dealing with every kind of tension.

Why is this a matter of trust? In dealing with tensions and transforming them back into creative energy, we begin to recognize that the energy of Life Itself has a will of its own. As we come to understand this, it becomes a question of trust for us to accept the outcomes determined by the energy of Life, even though we have no idea how things will turn out. Rather than trying to shape events according to our own will, we accept this total uncertainty in our lives and trust it. We could also say that we open ourselves to it.

Because we have this trust, slowly we allow Life Itself to reveal its highest inner content to us. This is also not easy. As things go along, our lives will present us with every opportunity to become disturbed. Instead we stay open.

This process has nothing to do with ordinary logic. It is not a reasonable process at all. Instead it is one of simply opening ourselves up and learning to trust. By dealing with tensions carefully, over and over again, and by cultivating a great skill in doing so, we learn to trust ourselves, we learn to trust other people, and we learn to trust Life Itself.

Moreover our trust is an expression of a profound respect for Life that allows the emergence of a genuine and universal love to permeate our minds, our emotions, and our lives. It is what allows us to become completely established in the original meaning of this experience, which is happiness. In other words, it allows us to become and remain happy.

In this state of trust, nothing can happen to cause us any real harm. Everything that happens becomes not a question of winning and losing, of gain and loss, or even of getting and giving away. It is really an issue of Life Itself articulating its own inner nature to us, nourishing and nurturing us in the understanding and awareness of its infinite potentiality for change and its infinite capacity for happiness.

We may have lived lives that have left us feeling there is no real reason to trust anything or anyone — that ultimately there is no help, and that nothing really supports us in our lives. We may experience the world as a fundamentally untrustworthy place.

Yet for all the difficulties we have undergone — all the ugliness and brutality — *something* deeper has allowed us to survive all that. Life Itself somehow has carried us this far. So whatever it was that got us this far and enabled us to survive our experience, we can start out by trusting *that* inner resource, because it is the deepest resource of all. It is the very foundation and essence of our strength. Then we can begin to look around and see how that same essence is expressing itself in infinite ways around us. Gradually we can learn to trust it more broadly and deeply. Eventually we recognize it in everything, because it is really all there is.

Deeply trusting that essence of Life Itself uplifts us beyond the confines of space. It removes the boundaries of time. It dissolves every kind of biological limitation, and puts us in touch with an extraordinary power — a power that is obscured only by the presence of insecurity, and the crystallization of that insecurity in the form of tensions. This power is what I mean when I talk about the divine.

This is a process that builds on itself. The more we decide to trust — and it *is* something we decide to do —

the more we allow the presence of the divine to permeate our awareness. Reciprocally, the more we open our awareness to the presence of this power in our lives, the more we discover that it is ultimately trustworthy. In time, this trust becomes so powerful that not only does it complete our lives, but it facilitates and promotes the completion of others in their own lives. This is remarkable and fine.

Trusting Life Itself is the ultimate act of surrender. It is not a blind act of faith, but a faith that we have explored and tested time and time again, and that we have found to hold. This simple, complete, and honest trust in Life is also the ultimate act of love. It is the union of the highest philosophical principle and of the ultimate practical expression within the reach and range of our everyday lives. It is the ultimate personal sacrifice and the ultimate universal experience. It releases our need for any particular outcome or form, and allows us to accept from deep within ourselves the presence of the divine in all its aspects. Through this experience we discover that every occasion of real love and every aspect of true growing have always been a matter of trust.

# Nonattachment

*If everything in the world ultimately arises out of one reality — one vital force — then it is impossible for us to be detached. As we open ourselves more and more deeply to our lives, what we discover is our ever-increasing interdependence and our total participation in Life Itself.*

# Solitude

PERIODICALLY we run into opportunities to change and grow in a real way. These are the critical junctures, the turning points in our lives for which we practice opening our hearts every day. We practice so that when we bump into these critical points we are able to stay steady, centered, and thoughtful even as we pass through them.

Because of this it is probably a good thing to be a little bit comfortable with silence and solitude. This doesn't mean that we have to live lives of solitude; it *does* mean understanding that, in a very real way, each of us is alone in our own inner work. We can only do it for ourselves. Although we may share a lot about it with others in ways that make it more interesting and comfortable, I'm not sure that this makes it any easier.

If we don't develop the capacity to be simple and quiet within ourselves, we won't have the inner environment for self-reflection. Then we have no means of discerning the distinction between our words and our actions — something which becomes particularly important when we confront the possibility of powerful change. We all have ways of telling ourselves that we are this kind of person or that kind of person, and that such-and-such is our objective. We are not always so good at discerning the gap between what we say and what we actually do. When we can be simple and quiet, we are more likely to have some honest sense of the discrepencies between our talk and our actions. Then we are able to enter into our relationships with others on a basis of real integrity.

The capacity for solitude and self-reflection becomes critical at those junction points where we face the possibility for real change and growth. As we go more deeply into our own hearts, the range of our awareness starts to grow, and a subtle change in our perceptions begins to take place. We may come to a point where we recognize that what we have actually been pursuing has little to do with the ideals we've been articulating. We find that the things we've taken to be signs of growth really aren't.

When this happens, it is a wonderful time to pull back and rethink the whole event. In doing so, we release and dump out a lot of garbage. We let go of wasted motion, unproductive involvements and attachments, and mistaken ideas we have about ourselves, our lives, and other people. We just drop it all, becoming simpler and more focused on our growth.

The ability to bring about this kind of release really depends on our having learned not to be afraid

of solitude or self-reflection, and on our having cultivated a rapport with ourselves. Only then are we not
afraid to look at the reality of any situation. To meet
reality as it is and to live from our deepest awareness
of it is essential to all real love.

# Endings

$A$NY time we are struggling to have or to hold on to any relationship in our lives, that relationship will become overly important to us and we will continuously be in and out of balance with it. Then everybody involved will be constantly jerking each other around. Better to have something we are trying to do with our lives, like growing as human beings.

If we make growing our focus, then growing becomes the foundation for all our interactions. It makes it our job in the relationship to be open and loving all the time, even though this openness and love will take many forms. Sometimes being open and loving means saying directly to the other person, "Please stop that!" Sometimes it is saying, "Why are things working out this way? Could you please explain it to me?" Sometimes we have to say, "I can live with some of this, but not with any of that." Then the other person can say, "I'll try," and we can say, "Okay." There is a whole process of negotiation, and it goes both ways.

A balance in this process is not possible if we are too attached to holding on to the relationship in the first place. All we end up doing is getting into a stranglehold in which nobody has room to breathe easily or speak simply. When we can operate from the appropriate balance, however, there is a continuous give and take.

If we take care of our own inner work well, we will have something left over that we will naturally want to share with somebody else. This is a good thing. The problem arises if we start to share more than we've got, because then we run into a deficit. To recover from that kind of drain on our resources will require a whole pullback. In the meantime, the other person is likely to get upset, since he or she was accustomed to a certain kind of relationship, and now it's changed.

If we are to have a truly shared life, it has to be based on some common objectives and mutual respect. Mutual respect emerges as we see that both of us are actually able to do what we say, and as we understand what the other needs us to do. Then a real appreciation and respect can emerge. Respect precedes authentic love. Even though we may say, "I love you," we usually mean something else. That's fine, but real love takes longer to develop. It does not come easily or cheaply.

There is no reason for a genuinely creative and loving relationship to dissolve. It may need to undergo some reorganization, but that's something different. Relationships dissolve only when our egos get in the way, because our egos can kill just about anything — they're stronger than liquid drain cleaner. Any creative and loving relationship changes form in one way or another over time, but there is no reason for it to break if each of us takes responsibility for our own ego. When we do, the love in our lives can continue to grow and increase. That love then becomes a tremendous source of strength as we move through all the critical junctures that come upon us.

However things turn out, at every point along the way we have our own end to uphold. This is the most important thing. Whether or not the partnership works out, if we have done our own inner work within it, then we come away with total benefit. Even if it fails miserably, there is nothing bad about the experience as a whole, because we come away knowing we did the best we could.

Bear in mind that there are two ways of thinking about what "the best we could" actually means. One involves just walking away, *telling* ourselves over and over again we did the best we could, because we can't face the fact that we didn't. The other is the quiet awareness and certainty that we really *did* everything we could have. When this is the case, there is no doubt.

Everything starts, however, with the understanding that our inner work must be our first priority. Then if the relationship ends, we still have been true to what our lives are really about; if the relationship continues, it will flourish in the spirit of that same work.

Sometimes, though, no matter what we do, important relationships in our lives come to a close. When we separate from someone else, we enter into the possibility of two processes. The first of these is a healing process.

I'm not particularly concerned about the healing itself, because I know it will come. What I *am* concerned about, however, is the second process, which is a little different. This is the process of going beyond all the tension, energy, and chemistry unleashed in the context of the separation. I do not want this energy to re-structure itself in the same old ways as the healing takes place.

Anything that is ruptured is going to heal. The real issue is the understanding and state of being that we cultivate as this healing happens. It is something like breaking an arm. There are lots of ways to set it or not to set it. Our concern should be to think ahead to the condition of the arm after the whole thing is over.

I would like to think that the breaks in relationship that I have experienced have not increased my cynicism, my sense of personal rejection, or my rejection of others. I would hope they have been experiences that have deepened my understanding of myself, as well as my compassion for and understanding of all concerned.

When we are sitting there hurting, it may be hard to remember these things. But all that hurt is energy that has been released through the interruption of a pattern. It is now looking to restructure itself somehow. That's what got us into the relationship in the first place. Our creative energy, which is at first unformed, structures itself in the form of our different experiences. One way it does this is to manifest itself concretely as our relationships.

When a break occurs, we have to think about what all that energy is going to do next. I am not concerned about its forming a new pattern; that's a given. What I want is for it to be a pattern that is not more contracted and tight — which is what happens whenever we come away from the experience saying something like, "I am *never* going to let myself be hurt again!"

Of course, we all know that even that isn't true. We all say it, but none of us sticks to it. It's just that we then get tighter and tighter around the whole situation. I would like, instead, to see an extended capacity for sensitivity and caring come through these experiences. I would like to see a pattern that is not smaller and tighter, but one that is bigger and much more open.

In order to keep the pain and disturbance from setting up tighter patterns, we have to sit there and learn to manage the energy that is released by the break. That's what I call busting our guts. Maybe it won't be all that intense an experience — if we get away with not having it be really hard, that's wonderful. It may mean that it wasn't that important to us in the first place, or maybe we didn't expose ourselves to it as deeply as we thought.

But we should be prepared for any break to be intense and for it to require that we be strong and demanding of ourselves. If there is someone about whom we care deeply, then losing him or her will hurt. If we get away with one that was easy, we may end up thinking that it will always be easy, which is a mistake.

The best thing to do is be prepared to work at staying open all the time, especially when we don't want to. We want to be prepared to manage our own creative power, which is the source of every kind of personal growth. This, at some point, is what leads to the possibility of spiritual growth, although the two are not exactly the same.

It's easy for us to be demanding of others. "You didn't do this for me and you didn't do that." But what was it *we* didn't do? When we can look at that part of the equation, then we can really grow. When we can manage to ask ourselves such questions honestly, not sidestepping them with excuses like, "Yes, but of course the other person did this and that," then the relationships in our lives will take care of themselves.

Moreover if we are really serving the power of Life within us and our objective in every case is to grow as human beings, then there can be no failure in any experience. Rather there is only the continuous discovery of the immense power of love within us. As that power unfolds, the faces in our lives may change, but the love does not.

# The Fruit and the Tree

$A$T A certain stage, there is a benefit in attachment. For example, the flowers on a tree draw benefit from their attachment. From the flowers come fruit and the fruit matures through its attachment. Then it falls away quite naturally. It does not have to be torn from the tree.

Likewise, we don't have to go around trying to sever our own attachments. It simply isn't necessary. The problem arises when the natural period of our relationship or connection to someone is over. We have to know when the time is up and then let the connection go, instead of trying to carry it around with us.

In the same way, we have to know when to let go of the people who have been attached to us in some way. We can't sit around blaming them for their need to move on. A tree doesn't say, "Oh, that terrible fruit! It left me back there. It's bad and awful, and I hope it lands on the pavement!" That's not surrender in the least. Better simply to go forward.

There is no such thing as an inability to surrender, but what there may be is a certain lack of maturity in a particular area. Consider, again, the analogy of the fruit and the tree. A fruit matures as the tree absorbs energy and nourishment from its environment. It comes into fullness in its own time and then lets go. In our own lives, we go through similar cycles. The whole process is one we can anticipate from the beginning and for which we can be prepared. When it actually happens, there is no need to feel any shock or sense of loss, because even when something leaves us, we remain established in the very foundation of the process of Life Itself.

On one level we exist as separate entities in a material world, and undergo emotional and intellectual events that arise and fall away. But this is only the smallest aspect of our existence. The process itself need not obscure our awareness of the deeper reality. We do not have to get lost in all the coming and going. Instead we can be at peace within our deepest Self, connected to the source of it all. Then whatever comes and goes, we don't suffer from it. That it will go, we know. That something else will come, we also know. Underneath all that, we are settled inside, full of the vitality and joy of Life and free to be as we are.

To surrender something doesn't mean it is *going* to leave us; nor does it mean it *has* to do so. In fact, every time we surrender into the flow of real love, does it become less? Does it get smaller? No. Instead, it gets bigger, and we find ourselves more filled by it, again renewed from it. This is love's biggest paradox. So letting go is not like dropping something from our lives. Even when some things do fall away in the process, the essence and reality of the true connection are never lost.

# The Big Picture

$M$ ANY people talk these days about learning to be detached. I don't use the term "detachment" very much anymore, because I think it tends to imply that we can separate ourselves from something, whether it be a desire, a circumstance, a feeling, or a person. Essentially I don't feel that this represents a real state of affairs, because we cannot avoid our connection to anything else. All of us are intimately interconnected in Life Itself by the power of Life within us. No inherent separation is even possible.

Sometimes we say, "Oh, I'll just detach from this person, place, or thing." We think we can simply close ourselves off and pull back from the relationship. What is less evident to us is that we could just as easily be practicing denial, repression, or rejection, and calling it detachment. Therefore in my view "surrender" is a better word.

Surrender implies a letting go of our own tension, a dissipating of whatever subtle or intense feeling has obstructed the flow between us and somebody else. It means that we open our hearts and go beyond our sense of separateness, entering into the experience of our relatedness to all things. We move from a state of tension and identification with our differences to a much simpler but more intense participation in the underlying unity of all things.

If we and everything else in the world ultimately arise out of one reality — one vital force — then it is impossible for us ever to be really detached from each other. As we open ourselves more and more deeply to our lives, what we discover is our ever-increasing inter-dependence and our total participation in Life Itself. We don't find that we are further away from others, but that our horizons expand to become more and more inclusive. By entering deeply into the essence of ourselves we remain, at the same time, in full contact with the whole field of our lives. In that experience, we don't have to deny, reject, disconnect, or detach from anything.

At the same time, because our horizons are extended to the absolute limit of our potential, we are also not directly engaged in dichotomy or tension. Then all the issues, desires, and questions we have in our lives find their proper place. Because we try to work from the broadest perspective possible, we draw from this big picture the strength to make the difficult choices we some-times must make. This big picture is the basis for the logic of love.

Without this big picture, we are constantly strug-gling with the question of what is going to happen to us next. We are constantly being pulled and tugged by the whole network of energies in which we participate. If we focus on the big picture, however, we can then rediscover the balance between ourselves and all situations seen and unseen, known and unknown, and all those we cannot anticipate.

When we open ourselves to the big picture, we find an inner serenity and a quiet strength. As various circumstances and opportunities present themselves, we don't get caught up in our doubts and fears. Instead, we are able to ask ourselves, "This is an opportunity for growing in some way, so how can I promote it?" Then everything becomes much simpler, and maintaining our balance in the face of big changes is not so difficult.

Throughout all of this, we remain deeply engaged, but in a different way. We choose the level of our involvement and look for the way to promote the highest best interest of everyone concerned. This is an expression of our surrender; it is the demonstration of our love.

# Opening Up Our Lives

Usually we enter the different situations in our lives with some agenda, stated or unstated. On a practical level this can sometimes be useful, but it can also limit us in ways we don't intend. Why? Because if we think we know what we want when we start out, the only thing we've done is limit where we can end up. This is fine and appropriate from a worldly point of view, because any project in which we're involved needs some definition, goals, and limits. But in our inner work, once we think we know where we want to go we already begin to close down our possibilities.

Surrender is a matter of suspending your commitment to the ideas you have about yourself in order to witness the spirit within you and its capacity to uplift you materially, emotionally, and intellectually. This doesn't mean, however, that you abandon anything fundamental about yourself. Real surrender never means going against your basic grain. It only serves to open up your life and help you go beyond the constraints of your imagination.

Everything that manifests in our lives exists for only one reason: not to *teach* us how to surrender, but simply for us *to* surrender — for us to let go of it. There may be something that happens in the interim between when it comes into our lives and when we let go of it, but the bottom line is that we still have to let go. Then even if it sticks around for a very long time, we have redefined our relationship to it in a way that recognizes the inherent freedom of all concerned. If we don't understand this ahead of time, then we will discover that we have been limited in our outcomes. We accumulate more and more baggage, which only weighs us down.

Many situations will come and go in our lives. A few people will learn with us what life is about. Then all parties will demonstrate a state of surrender that allows for a real and vital longevity. Growth can take place which is long-term and deeply alive. But that long-term, deeply alive demonstration of the power of Life Itself is based on our ability to let go and stay open.

What I have just said is that real relationship exists based on surrender, not attachment. In fact, real love exists between people who are able to free each other. When we are not attached, there is no limitation to the range of expression that the creative energy of Life can exercise in our lives.

Every situation in our lives happens for us to surrender. We can either spend our lives learning what this means, or we can spend them becoming more and more contracted in one way or another. This is true in every case. We are either busy getting tangled up in every kind of emotional issue, or we are busy rediscovering our humanity, rediscovering love in our lives, and rediscovering the spiritual source of our existence. This process of rediscovery will always bring us back into the heart of surrender.

# Choosing Happiness

*The point is to find the joy within ourselves. Choosing to do this every day, we find in every relationship a love which enriches every life it touches.*

# Happiness

THE Shankaracharya of Puri, a spiritual master from India, once told my teacher Rudi that we can know we are on the right track in our inner work when we are really happy. In every way, it is the simplicity, joyousness, innocence, and sweetness of true happiness and its child-like quality that penetrate the thickness, complexity, and tension which all mind-born knowledge must inevitably become. This happiness is our real pathway to the divine and the barometer for the truth in our rapport with all our experiences.

When we find ourselves becoming entangled and complicated, struggling for this thing and that in any relationship — pursuing anything but the purity of love and happiness — then we are on the wrong road. Whatever we may think we're after, we have the wrong understanding of what's really happening.

In every way, the happiness that arises from our contact with our hearts is what matures as love. This is what uplifts us. Whatever odd and unusual places that love may take us — and it will certainly take us places we never imagined we'd ever go — it doesn't matter. We cling tenaciously to the purity of our intention and to the state of unconditional happiness within ourselves, instead of holding on to all the superficial lines of reasoning that so easily loop themselves around the events in our lives.

What we are doing is learning to let go of our worries. To do this in any real way requires all the discipline, skill, and surrender we can muster. In releasing our tensions, we let go of worries and, in the space where the worries were, we carefully observe and understand the flow of energy that fills it instead. Then we simply keep getting out of its way and allow it to flow freely.

The more we do this, the more we find our attention centered on this inner resource in ways that change our whole understanding of ourselves and that allow us to interact differently with the people, places, and things around us. It is our worries that keep our attention scattered in every direction. When we can address the same situations without the worry, then our whole experience of them changes.

In the moments when we are really happy, where is our awareness? It is on that happiness. It floods our senses, permeates our perceptions, and takes us back to our natural condition. It is the tension and worry in us that keep us tuned into the same frequency of tension and worry in everyone else.

Whatever is dancing in us is what we see dancing all around us. When we let go of worry and tension, there is only a dynamic stillness. In that stillness, we experience the whole world as light and awareness.

# A Position of Strength

$O$ V E R and over again, we confront different pressures in our lives. These pressures can make us feel more and more isolated. Our experience of pressure and isolation is what we call suffering, and we spend a lot of time trying to alleviate it. Yet our struggles to deal with that suffering and to resolve it never seem to work. The reason for this is that any decision we make or effort we undertake always ends up having something to do with the point from which we start out. In a way, the beginning and the end are not different, because the two are essentially connected.

This means that when we start out from pain and suffering or from pressure and isolation, we inadvertently reinforce the pressure and intensify our isolation. Moreover this is true not only in our personal relationships, but in every field of our endeavor. If we begin in fear, asking one version or another of the mantra of ignorance, we can only end up more afraid. The pain will continue to build and our suffering will increase. As we have seen, this is the inevitable outcome of the logic of survival.

It is a great paradox that the decisions we make based on our ordinary instincts and intuitions tend to make problems worse in the long run, and not better. There is only one resolution to this dilemma: to change the place from which we begin. How do we do that? In a way, it is simple. We start every endeavor from a position of strength. By this I don't mean that we get tough. Rather I mean that we change our orientation: We start every endeavor from a state of happiness within ourselves.

You may ask, "But how do I do that? What do I *do* to be happy?" The only answer is that you just do it. The only way to be happy is to *decide* to be happy. There is nothing arcane or mystical about this; it is a simple resolve. We decide to be happy no matter what. In the process of doing this, we discover that happiness goes to happiness and that, as we cultivate it within ourselves, it increases.

The simplest and most important thing to understand in our spiritual work — and really in our lives as a whole — is that we have the opportunity every day to choose what that day will be. *We* decide.

We can't say what will happen to us, but we *can* say where we will live within ourselves in relation to whatever does happen. We get to choose whether or not to be open — whether or not we will feel the essence of what is alive within us and feel the simple happiness of it. If we choose not to be open, then we've got worries, problems, tensions, and things to be afraid of, along with too much to do. *We* decide.

What is truly remarkable is the effect of choosing to let go and be happy every day. Instead of being attuned to problems, difficulties, and obstacles, our minds suddenly start to be attuned to reasons for being happy. Because we remember to make this simple effort to be open and enjoy ourselves every day, what grows in our lives are more and more reasons for that joy. It is really very simple. It involves nothing but our conscious wish to grow, and our determined effort to be open.

People see what they love. People who love money see opportunities to make money everyplace; people who love music hear music all the time. Whatever we love is what we see. Only when we love the truth and cultivate our love for it within our hearts do we see its spirit and essence within all forms. Then we see the real love within whatever we *think* we love. This is the source of our happiness.

This approach, of course, is not the way that most of us have been conditioned to look at things. Most of us learned at an early age to think of being happy in terms of acquiring certain things. "I'll be happy if I have a relationship, I'll be happy if I have more money, I'll be happy if I have a new television, or a car, or if my boss likes me."

Yet when we really think about it, there is no person, thing, or condition that can actually *make* us happy. Of course the flip side of this is that no person, thing, or condition can actually *make* us unhappy, either. Every happiness is within us already, because we alone have the power to create our own lives. This is our fundamental creative power. So at some stage, we may come to the point where we say to ourselves, "Well, I guess I might as well be happy, no matter what."

Making the choice to be happy does not mean we will never suffer misfortune, become seriously ill, or undergo pain again. We all have different atmospheres, opportunities, and raw materials with which to work during the different periods of our lives. Some periods present us with one kind of challenge, others present us with something else. Some are enormously difficult, some are profoundly simple, and others are periods of profound abundance.

None of this matters. If we can't handle the periods of difficulty or simplicity well, we will never handle the periods of abundance well, either. In some way, the simple periods in our lives are the most wonderful, because they give us the opportunity to really learn value. Ironically it is the abundant periods that can turn into the greatest disasters, because we haven't understood value and developed the skill to deal with this creativity well.

The fundamental key to living fulfilled lives is to be happy, no matter what. If our lives are to be wonderful, we will learn this and live it. Moreover if we can resonate happiness long enough, our whole life will take on that same resonance. We are the conductors, and we make the music. We set the beat, and then all of life organizes itself around the music playing within us. So instead of stomping around our lives beating out the time in army boots, we should be careful — and we should be genuinely happy.

I do not mean to say that this is easy. Humans beings are fragile and somewhat limited creatures existing in an often dim and brutal world where it is difficult to be happy. So while this is not a heavy endeavor, it is a real and serious one. While it is simple, it is not so easy to remember to do.

Still, our trip through this world is so short that, if we are not happy, we're going to miss it. When we're not busy struggling for something — when we can just stop for a minute, take a breath, and clear our heads — we see just how fast it all goes. If we don't take the extraordinary opportunity we have in this life to engage this happiness, embrace it, and allow it to embrace us, then the moment is lost and our opportunity to wake up has passed us by.

If we have nothing in the world but fullness in our hearts, we have everything. If we have everything in the world and are not happy, what do we have? Just a bigger mountain of garbage than the person next door. I don't mean that the things we pursue in this world aren't meaningful and valid to us, or that we shouldn't work with integrity, nobility, virtue, and courage. But whatever we confront in our lives, we want to do so from a position of real strength.

This strength is based on recognizing our inability to control what happens to us in this world, and therefore the importance to us of authentic happiness. We can influence the events in our lives to some degree, but since somebody else is usually throwing the pitches and may occasionally cheat, there is only so much we can do.

Whenever I hear someone say, "But that's not fair," I say, "You're right. It's not." Still this lack of fairness need not limit us, because at every moment we have inside us an extraordinary source of strength. If we cultivate that happiness and recognize the completeness that is within us — the completeness that is Life Itself — then the happiness within us matures into love.

Such love is beyond time. It is beyond the finite and the personal, even though we experience it as individuals. It is what endlessly gives of itself without ever being reduced. It creates from within itself without ever being dissipated. It is infinitely uplifting and endlessly in harmony.

# A Wonderful Life

NOBODY gets what he or she wants in life. Nobody. Nothing happens to us the way we wanted it to or expected it should. We are given few overt reasons to be joyful. Moreover for the majority of us nothing comes easily or accidentally — certainly not things of value. So it is important to understand that it is our ability to find something wonderful in each relationship and to cultivate it carefully that makes the difference. We do this by confronting the difficulties that exist in every situation.

Confronting difficulties does not mean accusing or blaming anybody else for anything. It does mean continuing to search for what is fine and true in all things. This is something we must do consciously. It doesn't come about by accident. Our ability to find something wonderful in ourselves, to hold to it and see it in everybody else, and to work to participate in it is what constitutes our conscious effort to make a wonderful life. Then whether our experiences are long-lasting or short-lived, each one becomes beneficial to us. In fact we don't even care which way they go, because we have something wonderful in each moment. In this way we go beyond the difficulty in our lives.

The bottom line is that our lives together become wonderful because we decide they are going to be that way, and work every day to *make* them so. It happens because we don't let anything divert us from that intent. If we are going to be willful about anything at all, it should be about eradicating our own negativity. We can be willful about *that*, and run it out of town.

What will tell us about the real nature of our relationships is our own determination to find and develop what is fine and special within our own lives, and to find these qualities within every other person by first embodying them ourselves. Paradoxically a lot of what walks in the door looking like a reason to get excited usually isn't. On the other hand, what walks in looking like a real drag often turns out to be something special. So in our minds we can rarely know ahead of time, and we should not be quick to judge by appearances.

We find something open in everybody by first being open to ourselves. We find something honest in others by first being honest with ourselves. We find something giving in other people by first being giving ourselves. This is how we make our lives something amazing. It doesn't necessarily mean we have to stay in a particular relationship forever. It does mean that the depth we cultivate in ourselves and our lives creates an environment in which everyone involved can grow.

Cultivating our own lives should not create a situation in which the people around us become more tightly bound; it should create a situation in which everyone has more space in which to live, and more freedom to express themselves rather than less. It is our energy and our surrender that will bring this about, and nothing else.

Nothing in our lives lasts forever. Each thing appears for a while and then passes on. Yet far from being a cause for regret, the point of each of these appearances is to enjoy them. I find that I can sit by the ocean and watch it for hours. The rise and fall of the waves is endlessly changing. As the seasons go by, the light changes. As the wind rises and falls, the reflection on the water is different and its color varies. As the humidity in the air changes, so does the color of the air. It's fantastic, and all of it is there to enjoy — not to get entangled in. We don't say, "Keep that one wave just the way it is forever — freeze it!" We just watch it while it lasts, taking deep pleasure in its rising and subsiding.

This is how we can also look at the rising and subsiding of the people, places, and things in our lives. It is only because we imagine that we *need* some things and should shrink back or run away from others that we lose our ability to enjoy them just as they are. Instead we are constantly thinking, "But what's going to happen to *me*?" We misunderstand what all this appearance is about, and either get caught up in fighting it, running away, or trying to hold on to it just as it is.

The point of our lives is to enjoy them — indeed to enjoy this life as a whole. This is the point of every day. I don't mean that we should go out and do things we *think* are enjoyable. That's a phony approach. The real issue is to grow and open up within ourselves. We open, and learn to enjoy everything that presents itself. We can do this as long as we find and hold on to our center, which is where we get to when we enter into our hearts.

When I was growing up in a little town in the center of nowhere, I learned that if I wanted to have any fun I had to make it happen myself. Nobody else was going to do it for me. This is always true. We have to take responsibility for our own happiness. We are responsible for what our lives become. What this means is very simple. Life gives us what appear to be many choices, but they boil down to one: Will we choose to be happy, or not? I ask this because being happy is something we *choose* to do; it has everything to do with the way we choose to live our lives.

As I said earlier, happiness is not based on the presence of any external circumstances or conditions. Rather it is based purely on the presence of the spirit within us and on our awareness of that spirit. We take our attention inside, open our hearts, and feel the happiness that is there all along.

This may seem like something beyond your experience. It may seem as though I am assuming something to be a fundamental part of you that may not appear to you to be there at all. It may feel hard to know how to translate it into your own life. I can only tell you that there is nothing complicated about it. It is truly as simple as opening your heart, making the choice to be happy no matter what, and coming back to that choice over and over and over again each and every day.

Some people have said to me, "Well, how do I know I'm not just talking myself into it? You tell me that the happiness is there all the time and that all I have to do is tune into it, but how do I know I'm not just making it up?" I would ask a question in return: If you go to a water faucet, turn it on, and the water flows out, did you make it up? I don't think so. It comes out because it was already there.

In the same sense, every single time we truly open our hearts, the joy we feel is the joy that was there all along. We don't usually notice it, because we get so caught up in everything superficial and external. We get distracted by our efforts to look for this joy in all the wrong places. Then, of course, the experience of it is denied to us.

When we experience this joy, however, our lives become something rich, and the love we feel within ourselves is something we feel for everyone. It is not like a personal love, but a broad and universal love we share with everyone. At the same time, it makes all our relationships special, because relationships are like arteries. If we fill them with love, then they carry the flow of that love; if we allow them to become clogged with tension and uncertainty, then we have yet another reason for heart failure.

The point is to find the joy within ourselves. Choosing to do this every day, we find in every relationship a love which enriches every life it touches. It is a vitality which transforms us all. Each time we experience it, it changes us for the better, even though it is not always painless. This is what is special about being alive; it is what is special about being human. It is also what makes being together with others special.

We choose this. The practice of opening our hearts is simply the activity we do every single day as an expression of our choice and our commitment to being happy. This is our responsibility. It is because we choose to live in a state of unconditional happiness that our desires are fulfilled completely and purely. Our awareness of the infinite oneness underlying all our experience becomes strong and, from that awareness, every action that emerges from within us is nothing but a manifestation of the power of love. It is an expression not of some desire or expectation, but of true caring.

Then the tensions we feel are not the signposts of our lives; they are not the boundaries. They are not even the expression of any particular limitation. Instead they are like the places in the ocean where two big currents meet or where the wind and the current run counter to each other. There is a tension that manifests itself in the water, which is sometimes quite powerful. I've seen a riptide stand up about ten feet tall, and it can get even bigger than that. Is that riptide the expression of some limitation or the manifestation of some problem? I don't think so. It is just the point at which two strong natural forces meet, and the expression of their merging is something incredibly dynamic and vital.

When we choose to be happy, no matter what, we still experience tensions. I am, after all, not talking about living a tension-free life. But these tensions are no longer the boundaries for anything. The riptide that opens in the ocean is not a boundary, nor is it like a wall. In fact it is an expression of the vitality hidden within the ocean. Even on a quiet day it can sometimes take place. So it is not a limitation. It is only the ocean interacting with itself, just as our tensions are the point where the individual and the infinite come together.

If we observe the pulsation of this union in a state of unconditional happiness, free of judgment, then we have the capacity to observe and participate in the unbroken unity of the creative expression of all that is. Then every action, every impulse, and every inspiration is something magic and amazing. All of it becomes an endless experience that reinforces the unconditional love that is the essence of our being.

# The Power of Life Itself

$L$ O V E means something different to everybody. Yet
the experience of unconditional happiness continuously
pulls us back to a consideration of this term. In examin-
ing our individuality and the relationship we have to
other individuals in the context of this happiness, we
can only come to some thought about ourselves and
love, some discovery of the meaning of love between
individuals.

It is a remarkable situation to discover what is infinite within our own existence — to recognize in a simple,
sweet way the infinite resource that exists within us, and
to see its unlimited capacity for unfolding, extending,
and transforming itself. To experience it breaks apart
every kind of rationality. It also has a tremendously sub-
versive effect on our capacity to respect order, because it
is constantly rearranging the order within us and around

us, whether we want it to or not. It is constantly reaching into, drawing out of, and reorganizing its own extraordinary creative expression.

The power of Life Itself within us does these things without any respect whatsoever for our personal timetables, and with no appreciation for what we think of as our personal wants and needs. Yet even as it overrides our individuality and is utterly disrespectful of those wants and needs, its power has the remarkable capacity to fulfill us more than we ever imagined was possible. It brings about the continuously renewed experience of something so special that it is impossible to wrap our minds around it or comprehend it in any way. We can only appreciate it and be quiet in its company.

In the beginning, we have to work to stay open. We are constantly aware of just how counter-intuitive it feels to do so. Yet as our ability to do this matures, the happiness we discover becomes a complete surrender to, and acceptance of, the profound uncertainty that is the nature of all creation. Although ordinarily we resist this uncertainty, the happiness within us is what allows us to expand our horizons and to absorb our awareness of the infinite more deeply into ourselves. We recognize the fundamental, eternal nature of our own being, and dwell simply and at peace in that all the time.

Then we see our bodies and minds for what they are — as nothing but strands of light. To experience the total continuum of that light means that time and space no longer have the same hold on us anymore. There is only one time, and that is now. There is only one state, and that is joyous. There is only one desire, and that is peace.

# Epilogue

*Try to think about love. Try to let go of your will and, from within yourself, have a vision of love that you can see. Let that vision of love become your eyes and ears, so that love is what you see and love is what you hear. Only then will you see easily what choices to make and how to decide things.*

# Epilogue

SURRENDER is our natural state. The more we reside
in that state, the more deeply the reality of our creativity,
freedom, and intrinsic joy becomes apparent to us. When
we know our own hearts, then we love whatever choices
we make in our lives, because love is really the source of
all our decisions. We don't do things we don't love; we
don't do things we cannot love. If we look into something
and see that it doesn't come from love or lead to love,
then what is the point of engaging in it in the first place?
It's a dead end.

How do we know what is love? The poet Rumi says:

> Be drunken with Love,
> for Love is all that exists.
> Where is intimacy to be found,
> if not in the give and take of Love?

If they ask what Love is,
say, the sacrifice of will.
If you have not left will behind,
you have no will at all.

In a way, this may not seem practical. If it doesn't,
it is because usually we are trying to analyze, think, and
be reasonable about our choices. But if we step back from
any decision-making process, we see that there are no
reasonable choices in this world. We only make them
look reasonable to justify whatever we have decided.
The truth is that much of what we do is simply not reasonable. So why try to pretend that it is?

Try to think about love. Try to let go of your will and,
from within yourself, have a vision of love that you can
see. Let that vision of love become your eyes and your
ears, so that love is what you see and love is what you
hear. Only then will you see easily what choices to make
and how to decide things.

When we love like that, Life is nothing but the
unfolding of love, and we don't see anything else. We
don't see what is reasonable or not reasonable. All we
have to do is let go and let this knowing flow from us.
The love I am really talking about is universal love. What
is universal love? It is simply that fundamental awareness from which all experience emerges and into which
all experience subsides. It is love because it gives of itself
continuously and asks nothing in return. That is why we
call it love. It gives of itself endlessly, without ever being
diminished in any way, and its potential is infinite.

The surrender of our individual boundaries, our limited ideas, and our finite hopes and fears is the vehicle by

which we achieve this intimate, innate recognition of our own universal love. This is a process. The first part of this surrender involves being able to sit through the agitation and pain of letting go of these boundaries without acting out. It is what happens as we let the agitation slowly subside without flinching.

When we relax and get out of the way — when we surrender to the creative energy of Life Itself — then that potential will articulate itself the way that *it* wants. Even though this will have nothing to do with what we may have thought we wanted to do with our lives, it is still wonderful because we discover something brilliant within us that is bigger than we are. It is certainly bigger than our own imaginations. It makes our lives a process of discovery, and not a process of acting out everything that our parents, teachers, and the television have poured into our heads.

There is an amazing, infinite potential within us that is beautiful, joyous, and exhilarating to experience. A state of total well-being, it profoundly benefits those whose lives our lives touch. When we connect with that potential, our own experience of it is so rich that it transforms our experience of everything. We find ourselves giving easily and freely, without concern for what anyone does in return.

Of course when we talk about surrendering to the creative energy of Life Itself, we are also talking about opening to infinite uncertainty, because infinite uncertainty and infinite potential are the same thing. As long as we are talking about potential, we are talking about something that is not fixed.

Why is it that it scares us so much to recognize this uncertainty? Reason number one is that it puts us in our place. We see how infinitely small we are. Reason number two is that the parts of us that are temporary and programmed for self-preservation — our bodies and minds — resist it wildly.

Yet dealing with tensions and learning that we can, in fact, surrender and rise above them allows us to cultivate a deep trust in Life Itself. The strength of this trust, in turn, makes it possible for there to emerge from within us a capacity to serve whatever situation we find ourselves in. This service is really the creative activity of connecting and weaving the inner and the outer, until they reveal themselves to be a single fabric.

Finally we begin to listen to and hear the pulsation of Life Itself. We observe it as it explains to us its own nature. It begins to reveal to us our subtle connection and interdependency with all things. It discloses the warp and weft of all experience as a single fabric and we find our place within the whole, instead of experiencing a basic sense of isolation or separateness.

Surrender is the process of continuously releasing any experience of isolation or duality. The perception of isolation is something we often identify with and nurture in many ways. It is also the great cause of our frustration and suffering. It is, finally, the one thing we must surrender in order to experience the true depth of our own hearts.

It is the continuous opening within ourselves that allows us to examine what is taking place within our inner spirit. What we find there begins to show us directly the subtle connection that exists between ourselves and every other. There is a subtle unity that becomes increasingly clear to us — the subtle unity of all relationships. When we know this, we know our inner Self.

Over and over again the activities of the mind obstruct the calm and stability arising from our recognition of the unity with our inner Self. To clear that obstruction, we must surrender. Surrender, in this case, means becoming completely relaxed and open. Furthermore in surrender there is no grasping for any kind of understanding, idea, or concept. We are simply centered within ourselves in a state of complete openness to Life Itself.

Surrender means we are not reaching for anything else in that moment. Ultimately it means we are not reaching for anything at all. To become fully established in a state of surrender means that we recognize the perfection implicit in that inner spirit. From this awareness we completely accept ourselves, and come to a new level of acceptance toward our circumstances. The struggle doesn't exist anymore. There is only the effort to be aware of the presence of this spirit — our inner Self — all the time, and to allow that spirit to guide us.

This is a profoundly simple condition, free of attachments and desires, free of likes and dislikes. It is also free to recognize the potential of each moment and participate in it fully, without concepts or judgments, without ambitions or expectations. In that state, we are not immobilized; rather we are free to see clearly each new form of creative energy that presents itself. Then we are free to explore the infinite possibility, implicit harmony, and total freedom inherent in our lives. This is the flowering of the logic of love.

# ABOUT THE AUTHOR

$S$WAMI Chetanananda, also known as Swamiji*, is a highly respected American meditation master initiated in the ancient Saraswati order of monks, in the lineage of Bhagavan Nityananda of Ganeshpuri, India. He has instructed students for nearly twenty years in the practice of Trika Yoga, a branch in the tradition of Kashmir Shaivism, which promotes the integration of body, mind, and spirit. In this way, he has carried on the teaching transmitted to him by his own teacher, Swami Rudrananda, or Rudi.

As an American, Swamiji brings to his writing and teaching an extensive and deep personal experience of an Indian tradition gained through years spent traveling and studying in India, as well as his experience of

---

* The term "Swami" means "master of oneself." It also refers to his being an initiate of the Saraswati monastic order of India. "Ji" is a term of love and respect.

transmitting that tradition in an American context. He is well-versed in presenting his thoughts on inner work and spiritual growth in a down-to-earth American idiom accessible to a broad audience. In addition, he is familiar with the discourse and spirit of ancient Eastern spiritual texts. His understanding therefore cuts across cultural boundaries to make the spirit of the East accessible to people of all cultures, and his work suggests the ongoing vitality of the teacher tradition.

Born in Kentucky, Swamiji grew up in Indiana and went to Indiana University. In 1971 he went to New York to meet Rudi. Upon Rudi's passing in 1973, Swamiji undertook the direction of the spiritual community established by Rudi. This became the Nityananda Institute, a non-profit center dedicated to supporting individuals in the active practice of a spiritual life. In 1982, Swamiji moved the Institute to Cambridge, Massachusetts, where he currently resides.

The Institute has many facets: a community of over a hundred residents; a full schedule of hatha yoga classes; twice-daily meditation sessions (introductory class required); periodic workshops in meditation techniques, relaxation techniques, and health enhancement; programs of art and music; quarterly weekend retreats; public programs with Swamiji on Sunday mornings; and a wide range of publications by its associated publishing house, Rudra Press.